superhero
sewing

superhero sewing

Playful, Easy-to-Sew
and No-Sew Designs
for Powering Kids'
Big Adventures

LANE HUERTA

Creative Publishing
international

Brimming with creative inspiration, how-to projects, and useful information to enrich your everyday life, Quarto Knows is a favorite destination for those pursuing their interests and passions. Visit our site and dig deeper with our books into your area of interest: Quarto Creates, Quarto Cooks, Quarto Homes, Quarto Lives, Quarto Drives, Quarto Explores, Quarto Gifts, or Quarto Kids.

Text © 2017 Quarto Publishing Group USA Inc.
Project designs © 2017 Lane Huerta
Lifestyle photography © 2017 Lyn Bonham

First published in 2017 by Creative Publishing international, an imprint of The Quarto Group,
401 Second Avenue North, Suite 310, Minneapolis, MN 55401, USA.
T (612) 344-8100 F (612) 344-8692 QuartoKnows.com

Creative Publishing international titles are also available at discount for retail, wholesale, promotional, and bulk purchase. For details, contact the Special Sales Manager by email at specialsales@quarto.com or by mail at The Quarto Group, Attn: Special Sales Manager, 401 Second Avenue North, Suite 310, Minneapolis, MN 55401, USA.

10 9 8 7 6 5 4 3 2 1

ISBN: 978-1-58923-944-9

Digital edition published in 2017
eISBN: 978-1-63159-415-1

Library of Congress Cataloging-in-Publication Data available

Design: Think Studio | thinkstudionyc.com
Page Layout: Sporto
Photography: Lyn Bonham and Lane Huerta

Printed in China

For Clementine

contents

1

sewing essentials...10

2

superheroes...30

3

pirates...52

4

fairy queen and dragon king...66

5

magicians...82

6

woodland creatures...98

preface

We tell our kids they can be anything they want as long as they can imagine it. At Lovelane Designs, we want to help young imaginations soar all day long—and keep them dreaming at night. We know playing dress-up isn't about fitting into ready-made roles; it's about creating our own.

When I started screen-printing Lovelane's capes in a shed back in 2006, I wanted to inspire magical stories spun from the clouds and fantastic forts constructed from bedsheets. Now, with a daughter of my own, I've been lucky enough to experience plenty myself. The joy I feel when Clementine puts on something I've made and flies off in character is the best feeling. Ever.

In sharing the patterns for some of Lovelane's fanciful everyday playwear, I hope that you feel that same joy and pride. I see this book as a guide that not only helps fashion high-quality playwear projects but also helps create lasting memories with the favorite kids in your life. The patterns, instructions, and adorable images will show you how to make a superhero, a magician, a pirate, a fox, a bunny, and an enchanted king and queen for endless possibilities—just add imagination!

As you cut and sew these characters, keep in mind that nothing has to be perfect. What's most important is the love that goes into making each piece—and some of these projects are simple enough that your child can help, too.

So grab your scissors and thread, and let's see what happens when imaginations soar!

1

sewing essentials

No complicated patterns, no long list of supplies, no expensive fabrics, and no special sewing skills—just a few easy sewing techniques, lots of imagination, and a little of your time for a whole lot of fun!

basic tools

You only need a few basics to create all the projects in this book.

Basic Tool Kit

As long as you have a sharp pair of fabric scissors, you can get started! Of course, it does help to have a few other things. Grab an empty basket and pull together this short list of supplies and you'll be ready to get creative.

- Fabric scissors
- Hand sewing needles
- Iron and ironing board
- Pins and pincushion
- Ruler or seam gauge
- Seam ripper
- Small scissors or thread snips
- Thread
- Water-soluble fabric pen
- Pinking shears (optional, but really great to have)

Measuring

You'll need a variety of measuring tools, both firm and flexible.

- *Tape measure*. For measuring your little ones.
- *Yardstick* and *transparent ruler*. For measuring fabric before cutting, and for drawing straight lines when tracing the patterns (see opposite).
- *Seam gauge*. For measuring seam allowances and hems.

Cutting

Scissors are kind of like shoes; there is one for every occasion. You don't need all the scissors listed below, but you might want them.

- *Fabric scissors*. Your grandma was right: Invest in a good pair and use them only to cut fabric and thread.
- *Pinking shears*. These special scissors have an oversized serrated blade that creates a zigzag edge that keeps fabric from fraying.
- *Crafting scissors*. For cutting your copies of the paper patterns that are included with this book.
- *Small scissors with two sharp points*. For detailed work, like cutting threads or trimming away excess fabric.

- *Rotary cutter* and *cutting mat*. These are an excellent investment. They make cutting straight and curved lines super easy. Rotary cutters are very sharp and must be used with a cutting mat.
- *Seam ripper*. Cuts thread when you need to undo some stitching. This is one tool you might never need, but it's always handy to keep one at the ready if you do. Only for emergencies!

Working with the patterns

This book includes all the patterns you'll need to create each project. You'll find some of them on pages at the back of the book, as well as on two large sheets in an envelope at the front. You'll want to make your own templates or copies of the patterns so you can use them over and over again. See page 18 for guidance on how to work with the patterns provided.

- *Tracing paper*. A roll of tracing paper, preferably an extra-wide roll, rather than sheets, to create templates from the patterns in this book.
- *Lightweight cardboard*. In addition to tracing paper, you can use lightweight cardboard to make the templates for the appliqué patterns,
- *Pencil and eraser*
- *Water-soluble fabric pen*. To copy pattern markings onto fabric. **Before ironing, the markings must be removed by dabbing them with a clean, damp cloth; otherwise, they will become permanent.**

Stitching

Whether you're sewing by hand or machine, it's a good idea to familiarize yourself with how a sewing machine works. Keep the owner's manual handy; it shows the correct way to thread the machine and how to make a bobbin. See pages 26–27 for hand and machine sewing techniques.

- *Sewing machine.* Just a good old straight stitch home sewing machine will work.
- *Sewing machine needles.* Universals are the best.
- *Hand-sewing needles.* You'll need sharps for hand stitching.
- *Thread.* Cotton/polyester thread is a good all-purpose thread, suitable for making all of the projects in this book. Choose a color that matches or is slightly darker than the fabric you're sewing.
- *Iron and ironing board.* Your iron will need multiple heat settings and a steam option.
- *Walking foot.* This sewing machine attachment is used to sew fabrics that tend to slip or pucker, and for sewing through multiple layers of fabric.

Tip

A point turner, used to push out the points of corners, collars, cuffs, and other tight spaces, is a handy tool. However, if you don't want to invest in one, a chopstick works just as well.

No-sew projects

While almost all of the following products are machine washable, you should check the label for care and application instructions, especially if you like to throw everything in the washing machine! See page 29 for more detailed usage and application tips.

- *Fabric glue*. Heat-set fabric glue is a great product for tackling no-sew projects. Although I'm partial to needle and thread, heat-set glue can hem projects quickly while maintaining the original flexibility of fabric. It's not suitable for permanent seaming, but perfect for hemming, attaching patches, appliqués, and trims.
- *Fusible adhesives*. There are a variety of different sheet-type adhesives used to bond layers of fabric without sewing. They're sold with adhesive on one or both sides and are secured through the application of heat, steam, and pressure. They're especially useful for attaching appliqués and for making hats, crowns, masks, and other accessories. They're sold in sheets, in rolls, or by the yard in fabric and crafts stores.

- *Fusible interfacing*. This textile product is fused to the wrong side of a fabric to add support and/or to stiffen it. There are many weights. Try to match the interfacing weight to the weight of the fabric. If the fabric is thin, choose lightweight interfacing. Felt typically doesn't need interfacing unless it's very thin, lightweight felt.
- *Spray adhesive*. Spray adhesive creates a temporary bond to hold trim in place while you sew it.
- *Liquid seam sealant*. This colorless solution prevents fraying. It's perfect for finishing ribbon ends and the raw edges of fabrics that won't be hemmed.
- *Velcro®*. Velcro, or hook-and-loop tape, is super-easy to use and a great fastener for kids' wearable projects.

fabrics

One of the best things about making playwear is that it doesn't have to fit perfectly and you don't need to use expensive fabrics. Check the remnant table at your local fabric store or your own linen closet for old sheets and pillowcases. Here are some popular choices.

- *Broadcloth, shirting, or cotton prints* are inexpensive, easy to sew, and come in bright colors and fun prints.
- *Canvas* is usually made of cotton or linen. It differs from other cotton fabrics, such as denim, in that its weave is plain rather than a twill. It's a great way to create playwear that's ready for your little artist's creative touch (see page 69).
- *Costume satin* is 100% polyester and machine washable. It looks and feels like high-quality satin; perfect for fancy capes and anything that calls out for a shiny surface.
- *Felt* is wide, nonwoven fabric, usually made from wool and acrylic fibers. It has no grain and its cut edges won't ravel.

Medium-weight felt is best for wearables, heavyweight felt for accessories. Avoid lightweight felt because it tears easily. Iron felt on a low to medium heat setting.

- *Flannel* is soft, like pajamas, perfect for lining hats and capes.
- *Polar fleece* doesn't ravel; it's soft, warm, and easy to sew. It's also wide—either 54" (1.14 m) or 60" (1.52 cm)—so a yard (meter) of polar fleece gives you more fabric than one of a broadcloth or satin.
- *Sherpa* is soft and fluffy and resembles a sheep before it is shorn.

Fabric Tips

- *Choose fabrics that don't ravel,* like felt, fleece, and microsuede, so you won't have to finish the edges.
- *When choosing fabric for the capes,* keep in mind that lightweight fabrics like satin will swirl and twirl. Heavier fabrics, like fleece or felt, will be a bit stiffer, but the cape will keep your dresser-uppers super-warm. If you choose a fabric that doesn't ravel, then all you have to do is cut it out—no edge finishing necessary.
- *If you want to use a print fabric, follow this general rule of thumb:* The scale of the print should fit the project. Fabrics with larger motifs or widely spaced prints work better for larger items like capes, while fabrics with smaller motifs or more closely spaced prints are better suited to smaller projects like hats.

working with the patterns

The patterns included with this book are generally sized for kids between the ages of three and eight, but because they don't really need to fit, they're perfect for a lot of different sizes.

At the front of this book is an envelope with two large sheets of paper printed with many of the pattern pieces you'll need to create the projects. You'll find some of the smaller appliqué patterns on the last several pages of the book. The patterns are full size and include a ½" (1.3 cm) seam allowance.

So you can use the patterns over and over again, you'll make templates of the patterns for the projects you're sewing.

Measuring your kid

Since these aren't close-fitting garments, exact size isn't important, but you might want to make the capes a bit longer or shorter and the hats a bit smaller or larger.

1. Use a yardstick with the child standing against a wall for length and height measurements. Measure circumference with a tape measure.
2. Make note of the following measurements:
   • back of neck to knees (for longer capes)
   • back of neck to hips (for shorter capes)
   • wrist circumference
   • head circumference (for hats, crowns, and mask)

Making the templates

Keep the patterns intact for multiple uses by tracing them onto tracing paper, cardstock, oak tag, or lightweight cardboard to make templates. Transfer all informational markings from the patterns onto the templates, including notches, cutting directions, and openings for turning.

Before using the templates to cut out the fabric, you might want to alter them.

• *It's easy to shorten or lengthen the cape/ cloak templates.* Compare your child's measurements with the measurements of the templates (from the neck to the bottom edge) and adjust the template accordingly. Simply use a transparent ruler to measure around the bottom edge of the cape/cloak and either add or subtract the desired amount.

Fit suggestions

- *Use hook-and-loop tape to adjust the fit on the Superhero Cuffs and the Dragon King Crown.* By placing the hook-and-loop tape horizontally, you can make the wrist cuffs and the crown tighter or looser.
- *Make sure the hats fit and don't slip into your child's eyes.* Because it's a bit tricky to measure your child's head in exactly the right place, make the hats and then try them on. If the hat is too big, stitch a big tuck right up the center back of the hat. If it's too tight, cut an opening up the center back—but if the hat is made from fabric that ravels, you'll need to zigzag stitch on each of the cut edges.

Using the templates to cut the fabric

Once you've traced the patterns to make the templates and made any size adjustments, you'll want to refer to the cutting instructions for each of the projects.

- Sometimes the pattern represents only half the garment, so the template edge needs to be aligned with the fabric fold.
- Sometimes you need to flip the template so you cut the template plus a mirror image.

Be sure to read the notes on the patterns and the cutting instructions in the project directions.

helpful terms

This mini glossary will help you understand many of the basic sewing terms used in this book.

- *Appliqué*. A shaped patch of fabric that's sewn onto a base fabric for decorative purposes. Felt is the perfect appliqué fabric because of its clean, nonraveling edges.
- *Bias*. The bias grainline refers to the 45-degree angle (or diagonal) between the length and the width of woven fabric. This is the imaginary line on which the fabric stretches the most.
- *Backstitch*. Several stitches taken back and then forth at the beginning and end of a seam to lock the stitches.
- *Basting stitch*. A long, straight stitch with long spaces between each stitch; used to temporarily hold fabric layers or fabric and trim together.
- *Bond/bonding*. Joining two pieces of fabric together with fabric glue or a bonding agent, often applied with heat from an iron (see No-Sew Projects, page 15; and Fundamental Techniques, page 22).
- *Clipping*. Cutting fabric with small, sharp scissors within the seam allowance but not through any stitching.
- For an outer curve: Straight clip up to, but not through, the seamline.
- For an inner curve: Clip small V shapes to minimize fabric bunching when turning the fabrics right side out.
- For corners: Clip diagonally into corners.
- *Cut on fold*. Some of the patterns are only half the design, so they need to be cut on the fabric fold. Fold the fabric in half. The pattern will indicate which line on the pattern needs to be placed on the fabric fold. Cut around the template, except for the folded side of the fabric.
- *Edgestitching*. Visible stitching right near the edge of a finished piece.
- *Finger-press*. Use your fingers and pressure to open seam allowances (or press them to one side) that may not be suitable for pressing with an iron.
- *Marking*. Using a water-soluble fabric marking pen to draw stitching lines or important placement indicators directly on the fabric. Practice on scrap fabric to make sure the markings come off the fabric.
- *Notch*. A marking on a pattern to show where seams should meet for sewing.
- *Press cloth*. A piece of fabric that protects the sole plate of your iron when using fusible products. Place the press cloth between the fabrics and the iron. You can buy specific press cloths or make your own from muslin or other heavyweight, light-color fabric.
- *Pressing*. Using an up-and-down motion that doesn't stretch the fabric.

- *Right side of fabric (RS).* The printed side of the fabric, or the side that looks best.
- *Reverse appliqué.* An appliqué that features a cut out shape on the top layer of fabric to expose the layer below (see page 25).
- *Seam allowance (SA).* The fabric between the edge of the fabric and the line of stitching. In this book, all patterns feature ½" (1.3 cm) seam allowances.
- *Stitch length.* In general, regular sewing is about 8 to 12 stitches per inch (2.5 cm). The scale varies from machine to machine, so be sure and check your sewing machine manual.
- *Topstitching.* Longer, visible, and often decorative stitching on the right side of the fabric, about ¼" (6.4 mm) away from the fabric edge. Consider using contrasting thread color for a decorative touch.
- *Trimming.* Cutting away excess seam allowance to reduce bulk.
- *Turning right side out.* Turning an outer fabric and lining right side out after sewing the two layers with the wrong sides together so the seam is on the inside.
- *Universal needle.* A sewing machine needle with a slightly rounded tip suitable for sewing for woven or knit fabrics.
- *Wrong side of fabric (WS).* The non-printed side of the fabric, or the less attractive side.

fundamental techniques

There are several sewing and fusing techniques or processes that will help you with all your sewing projects, not just the ones in this book. Consider this section a primer on basic sewing skills.

Working with fabric glue and fusible products

Fusible products and fabric glue make it incredibly easy to create simple projects, with or without any sewing. You can bond two layers together, add stiffness or body to the fabric, or attach decorative trim and appliqués. See "No-Sew Projects," page 15, for a list of fusible products.

If you'll be sewing after attaching the fusible, look for a "sewable" fusible adhesive to avoid gumming up your sewing machine needle. Look for the terms "lightweight" or "sewable" on the end of the bolt or packaging.

You can use heavy-duty fusible web for no-sew projects. This product is firm and has extra adhesive for a stronger hold.

General guidelines for working with fusibles

These products are applied with a combination of steam, heat, and pressure, so you'll need a steam iron and a press cloth.

- *Follow the manufacturer's directions* printed on the packaging and always test any fusible on a scrap of the fabric you'll be using for the project.
- *Protect your iron* by positioning a press cloth between the fabric and the iron. Dampen the press cloth for extra steam.
- *Press fusibles*—lift and press the iron downward—don't glide or slide it. Gliding the iron can cause the fusible to bubble or the fabric to stretch. Press for 8 to 10 seconds and then lift.
- *If you're using a paper-backed fusible,* let the fabric cool and then try to peel one of the corners of the paper; if the paper doesn't come off, apply more heat and pressure and try again.

Tip
It takes a bit longer to fuse felt to itself or to another fabric. It also might require higher heat, so you really should fuse a practice sample before working on your project.

• *If you're fusing two fabric layers together,* try to separate the layers at one of the corners. If you can pull the layers apart, re-press them. Repeat until the layers are firmly bonded.

DOUBLE-SIDED FUSIBLE ADHESIVES

These products, which have adhesives on both sides, are available in different weights and with/without paper backing on one side. To use, sandwich between two fabric layers and bond the layers together. They're perfect for no-sew projects, securing appliqués in place prior to stitching (or even without stitching), and hemming.

Applying paper-backed, double-sided fusibles

It's easiest to apply fusibles in two steps so you can control the placement. Paper-backed fusible web allows you to press the web in place, remove the paper, and then position the trim or second fabric layer over the web and press again.

1. Draw your own design or trace the pattern provided onto the paper side of the fusible. Use a ruler for straight lines. Draw or trace quickly and smoothly, keeping in mind that you can always smooth the marked lines when you cut the final shape.
2. Cut around the drawn shape, leaving at least 1" (2.5 cm) all around, unless you are cutting straight strips to hem or attach trim.
3. Press the fusible, paper-side up, onto the wrong side of the fabric, following the manufacturer's instructions for heat and time. Generally, it only takes a few seconds to set the adhesive.

4. Cut along the marked lines.
5. Remove the paper backing.
6. Position the shape, adhesive-side down, on the right side of the foundation fabric and fuse it in place.

If you want to print a design from your computer, try fusible printer paper and apply it the same as paper-backed fusible adhesive.

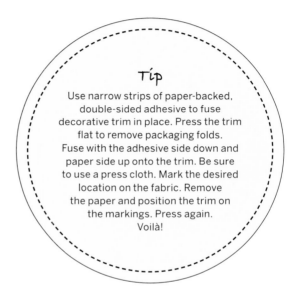

Tip
Use narrow strips of paper-backed, double-sided adhesive to fuse decorative trim in place. Press the trim flat to remove packaging folds. Fuse with the adhesive side down and paper side up onto the trim. Be sure to use a press cloth. Mark the desired location on the fabric. Remove the paper and position the trim on the markings. Press again. Voilà!

Applying double-sided fusibles without paper backing

1. Cut out the two layers of fabric and the fusible into the desired shape.
2. Layer the fusible between the two fabrics.
3. Press the fabrics together, following the manufacturer's instructions for heat and time.
4. Trim as needed.

FUSIBLE INTERFACING

Interfacing adds body, stability, and in some cases, stiffness to the fabric. It has adhesive on one side.

1. Place the interfacing adhesive-side down on the wrong side of the fabric. Cover it with a damp press cloth.
2. Use a dry iron on a warm setting and press (don't iron) one area for about 15 seconds. Lift and repeat until the whole piece is fused in place.

FABRIC GLUE

Fabric glue is okay for hemming and attaching small things, like beads, patches, appliqués, and trim, particularly if the item won't be laundered often.

Note that too much glue can soak through the fabric, so apply it with a light hand—you can always add more.

SPRAY ADHESIVE

Simply spray the adhesive in place to temporarily hold layers together so they're easier to sew. Use a light hand so the adhesive doesn't gum up your sewing machine needle.

The art of appliqué

It's amazing how colorful and playful fabric appliqués can make simple projects super-special.

Take a bit of time to choose your appliqué fabrics. Felt is perfect because it doesn't ravel. You can simply topstitch felt appliqués in place. However, pretty cotton prints or luscious silk shapes make great appliqués, too. You just might want to fuse them in place, then finish the cut edges with machine zigzag or hand stitches.

PREPPING APPLIQUÉS

1. Start every appliqué project by tracing your chosen designs, like the simple stars and lightning bolts used for the Superhero capes, onto tracing paper to make a template. You might even want to trace the designs onto lightweight cardboard or sturdy paper, like oak tag, so you can use them as templates over and over again.
2. Use the template to trace the design with water-soluble marking pen directly on the fabric (or on the paper side of fusible adhesive; see page 23).
3. Cut out the appliqué along the drawn outline, unless the project instructions indicate something different. (Some appliqués might need to be "rough cut," which means to allow extra fabric all around the marked lines.)
4. To remove the markings, dab them with a damp cloth.

TOPSTITCHING APPLIQUÉS

Follow these steps for perfect, one-step application, especially for felt appliqués:
1. Position the appliqué(s) on the foundation fabric.
2. Layer the appliqué pieces, if desired, as specifically indicated in each of the projects. Pin or spray baste them in place.
3. Topstitch the appliqué layers in place.

FUSING APPLIQUÉS

For this technique, you'll need a paper-backed, double-sided fusible adhesive (see page 23). If the fabric doesn't ravel too much, you only need to fuse it in place. However, if the fabric does ravel, or you want to add another design element, you can machine- or hand-stitch around the outer edge of the appliqué. You can even outline the appliqué edge with fabric paint or zigzag machine stitches to minimize raveling.

1. Trace the appliqué onto the paper side of the adhesive. Do not cut around the drawn outline; leave at least ½" (1.3 cm) all around.
2. Place the adhesive paper side up on the wrong side of the appliqué fabric. Fuse it in place following the manufacturer's instructions.
3. Cut out appliqué on the marked outline.
4. Peel off the paper. If it's hard to separate the edge of the paper backing from the fabric, insert a pin into the center of the design and make a small tear. Continue tearing to help remove all the paper backing. Position the appliqué on the foundation fabric, and fuse it in place.

Hand-stitching a fused appliqué

Blanket stitch around the raw edges (see page 26). This stitch tends to protect the raw edges and gives a really neat finish.

Machine-stitching a fused appliqué

Many sewing machines will have a blanket stitch setting, or you can machine zigzag. Start stitching in an inconspicuous place, like a corner, or a place that might be covered with a button, bow, or second layer.

Adding accent stitching

Draw any accent lines or other design features on the front of the appliqué with the water-soluble pen, then machine-stitch directly over the markings.

For raw-edge appliqué

This application doesn't hide the cut edges of the appliqué and encourages a frayed edge. If you plan to fuse the appliqué in place, trim the fusible ½" (1.3 cm) smaller all around than the appliqué, or you can straight stitch the appliqué in place at least ½" (1.3 cm) from the cut edge.

For reverse appliqué

Reverse appliqué features a design or portion of the top layer of the appliqué cut away to reveal the background fabric (or bottom layer of the appliqué). It's really easy when you use felt because of its clean cut edge. A woven fabric will, of course, fray a bit at exposed edges.

1. Trace the templates onto the appliqué fabric and cut them out, leaving about 1" (2.5 cm) around the marked outlines on all sides. Trace the design lines (for the cut out) on one of the appliqué pieces.
2. Layer and pin the two appliqué pieces together.
3. Topstitch over the interior design lines. Trim away the excess fabric by cutting ⅛" (3 mm) from the outside marked lines, and then topstitch the appliqué to the foundation fabric.
4. Cut *through the top layer only*, about ⅛" (3 mm) from the edge of the interior stitching lines, and remove the interior section of the top fabric to expose the bottom layer of fabric.
5. Be sure to remove the marked lines from both layers of fabric by dabbing them with a moistened cotton ball. ***If you iron the fabric before removing the marks, they will become permanent.***

Hand stitches and supplies

Sewing by hand is the perfect way to teach yourself and young children how to sew. All you need is a hand needle and thread. Of course, you can always use fusible products or a sewing machine instead of hand sewing.

HAND NEEDLES & THREAD

- *Hand sewing needles are sized from 1 to 26;* the higher the needle size, the finer and shorter the needle.
- *Sharps* are all-purpose, medium-length needles, and are perfect for most stitching.
- *Embroidery or crewel needles* have a sharp point and larger eye and are used for decorative stitching with thicker thread.
- *All-purpose cotton/polyester thread* is suitable for most hand and machine sewing.
- *If you're stitching decoratively, use embroidery floss*, which has six thin strands twisted together. The strands can be separated. For a heavy-looking stitch, use six strands; for a lighter look, separate the floss into two or three strands.

HAND STITCHES

Thread the needle with an 18" (45.7 cm) length of thread and knot one end, or secure the thread to the fabric with one or two small backstitches taken in the same spot. Many of these same stitches can be done with a sewing machine, too.

- *Backstitch.* A strong stitch that resembles machine stitching, backstitching is perfect for seaming. Working from right to left, take a stitch back ⅛" (3 mm) to ¼" (6.4 mm) forward on the seamline. Continue so stitches overlap with no spaces between them.
- *Basting stitch.* This long stitch holds fabrics together temporarily. Make evenly spaced, long stitches about ½" (1.3 cm) long with ½" (1.3 cm) between them.
- *Blanket stitch* (see below). Perfect for hand-stitching appliqués when the fabric ravels. Insert the threaded needle the desired distance away from the fabric edge and bring it out at the fabric edge with the thread underneath the needle. Pull the thread gently so it forms a thread edge along the fabric edge. Repeat with evenly spaced, even-length stitches.
- *Slipstitch.* Almost invisible, this stitch is used for hems and to hand-sew openings closed. Slide the needle inside the fabric fold and then out into the adjoining fabric fold. If you're hemming, alternate the stitches from the fabric fold to a thread of the fabric opposite.

Using a sewing machine

Practice stitching on scrap fabric to make sure the machine is stitching properly. As a general rule, a setting that creates about 8 to 12 stitches per inch (2.5 cm) is best for most sewing. If the fabric is heavy and bulky, you can use fewer stitches per inch (2.5 cm). If the fabric is lightweight, you might need a shorter stitch length.

SEWING A STRAIGHT SEAM

A seam holds two fabric pieces together. The seam allowance is the fabric between the actual seam and the cut edge of the fabric. All the seam allowances in this book are ½" (1.3 cm) unless otherwise noted.

1. Pin the fabric layers together, with raw edges even and right sides facing, unless otherwise noted. Place pins perpendicular to the cut edge (see A).
2. Set the sewing machine stitch length between 8 and 12 stitches per inch (2.5 cm).
3. As you begin stitching any seam, hold the thread tails so they don't tangle.
4. Take a few reverse stitches at the beginning and sew the seam.
5. At the end of the seam, take a few more stitiches to secure the stitching. Raise the needle and presser foot and clip the threads close to the stitching.

ZIGZAG STICH

This is a basic stitch available on almost every machine (see B). It's perfect for stitching the raw edges of appliqués. You can also use it along the cut edge of fabrics that ravel as decorative topstitching or to attach trim by machine. Check your owner's manual for details. You'll need a general purpose or zigzag presser foot for this stitch.

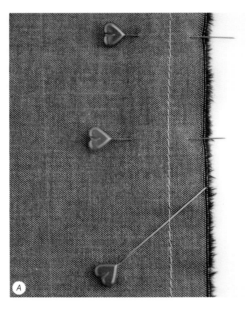

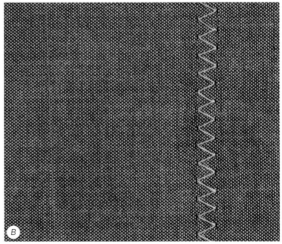

use your superpowers

Everything is optional! Use this book as a jump start to fill your child's dress-up box with fun, creative, and totally awesome original options. The only limit to what you can create is your imagination.

- *Find fabric you love.* There are so many fabulous prints and textured fabrics! Just walk into a fabric store or browse online and enjoy the vast choices.

- *Play with color.* It's amazing how the same thing can look so different just because it's a different color. And remember to add a different color or patterned lining for an extra dash of color.
- *Add any kind of embellishment.* The more feathers, fringe, ribbons, gemstones, fabric paint, and anything else you can find in the dollar or craft store, the more magic!
- *Look in catalogs, magazines, and online for more dress-up ideas,* and use the patterns in this book over and over again.
- *Ask your kids how they want to make their playwear their own.* They're usually filled with exciting ideas.
- *Try starting with a blank canvas,* and paint your fabric. See page 78 for details.
- *Cut up old blankets and sheets to use as fabric.* It's a great way to upcycle!
- *Change the length to change the mood.* Longer capes can be villainous or fairy princess like, and shorter capes are perfect for dashes through the woods to grandmother's house.
- *Make an assortment of magic wands.* Even Superheroes and Pirates could use a little magic!

caring for your playwear

Remember, these wearables are made for playing, so they're going to get dirty—and that's okay.

- You can put many of these projects right in the washing machine, but you might want to avoid the dryer. Heat can be hard on clothing! Line drying will extend the life of your playwear.
- Avoid putting felt items in the laundry. Brush them off or dab them with a little soapy water. You can remove grease stains with a little cornstarch.
- If you used adhesives and didn't sew the playwear, you might want to hand wash the items so the abrasion from the washing machines doesn't weaken the adhesive bond.

- If you are using cotton fabrics, just throw the pieces in the wash—even if they fray a bit, it's okay.
- The fabric hats should be okay in the wash, but those with felt appliqués would do better with a lighter touch—a brush or spot cleaning.
- As long as you remembered to heat-set your fabric-painted pieces (see page 79), they can go in the regular laundry.
- Note that the painted Fairy Queen and Dragon King wings have a layer of batting, so you should wash them on gentle, the same as you would wash a quilt.

superheroes

Everyone loves a superhero!
From a mask to a cape, these
super pieces will have your
super one dreaming big and
saving the world. What's his
or her superhero power?

getting ready to sew

Capes and accessories will transform your little ones—and even the family dog—into superheroes!

I used a traditional palette of pink, white, and red for one cape and a high-contrast mix of traditional (blue and white) and unexpected (orange) for the other. Feel free to make your own color choices and to switch up the appliqués if you—or your little superhero—would like.

Instructions are provided for capes, a mask, a hat, and wrist cuffs.

WHAT YOU'LL NEED

Basic tool kit (see page 12)

Templates (see Patterns, opposite)

FABRICS AND NOTIONS

Fabric suggestions:

For the capes: medium-weight cotton, lightweight cotton canvas or heavyweight muslin, denim, chambray, or kona cotton

For the hat: heavyweight cotton or cotton canvas, denim, solid or small graphic pattern. Be mindful with stripes and larger patterns.

For hat lining: cotton, shearling, felt, fleece, flannel

For mask, cuffs, and appliqués: felt

For the kid's cape:

1 yard (0.9 m) of 45" (1.14 m) wide fabric for the right side of the cape

1 yard (0.9 m) of 45" (1.14 m) wide fabric for the lining

3" (7.6 cm) of ½" (1.3 cm) wide Velcro/hook-and-loop tape

For the sidekick cape:

1 yard (0.9 m) of 45" (1.14 m) wide fabric for both fabric and lining

Optional: 1 yard (0.9 m) of twill tape

For the cape appliqués:

For the shooting star: ⅓ yard (30.5 cm) each of felt in four colors

For the lightning bolt: ⅓ yard (30.5 cm) each of felt in two colors

For the mask:

½ yard (23 cm) of felt

For a reversible mask, ¼ yard (0.5 m) pieces of felt in two different colors

Iron-on adhesive (Thermoweb Heat'n Bond Lite Iron-on Adhesive, 4" x 36" [10 x 91.5 cm])

For the hat:

½ yard (0.5 m) of 45" (1.14 m) wide fabric for the hat

½ yard (0.5 m) of 45" (1.14 m) wide felt or fleece for the lining

Use felt or fleece for the lining to help the hat stay on and keep little heads warm.

For the hat appliqués:

For each shooting star: 5 felt remnants large enough to cut 2 stars/3 flares

For each lightning bolt: 3 felt remnants large enough to cut 3 lightning bolts; handful of polyester fiberfill

For the cuffs:

For the shooting star cuffs: 6 pieces of 10" x 12" (25.4 cm x 30.5 cm) felt remnants in 3 colors

For the lightning bolt cuffs: 6 pieces of 10" x 12" (25.4 cm x 30.5 cm) felt remnants in 2 colors

4" (10.2 cm)-long piece of Velcro/hook-and-loop tape for each cuff

PATTERNS

Trace the pattern pieces for all the projects you intend to make, including the appliqués, onto tracing paper or lightweight cardboard according to the instructions on page 24. Be sure to copy any pattern markings, such as

notches and placement indicators, onto the templates. Cut out the traced patterns to make reusable templates.

PATTERNS ARE PROVIDED FOR THE FOLLOWING ITEMS:

Kid's cape (pattern sheet 1)

Sidekick (dog) cape, in 3 sizes (pattern sheet 1)

Hat gusset (pattern sheet 2)

Hat side (pattern sheet 2)

Mask (pattern sheet 2)

Cuffs (page 113 and pattern sheet 2)

Appliqués (pages 115, 117, 119, and pattern sheet 1)

Tracing the patterns and cutting the fabrics

1. Both the kid's and dog's cape templates need to be positioned on the fabric fold (see pages 19 and 20).
2. Pin the templates on the fabric or felt as follows and cut out the fabric. Note that the shape for center front of the center hat piece is different for the superheroes/bunny and the fox. There are two cutting lines indicated on the pattern; use the gently inward curved solid cutting line.
   - *Cape:* Cut 1 from fabric and 1 from lining
   - *Dog cape:* Cut 1 from fabric and 1 from lining
   - *Hat gusset:* Cut 1 from fabric and 1 from lining
   - *Hat side:* Cut 2 from fabric and 2 from lining
   - *Mask:* Cut 2 in different colors of felt
   - *Shooting star cuffs:* Cut 6 from felt: 2 of the main color and 2 of each accent color.
   - *Lighting bolt cuffs:* Cut 6 from felt: 4 of the main color and 2 of the accent color.

   If you're using woven fabrics instead of felt, be sure to cut 1 of each piece and then flip the pattern to cut the others so you have mirror images.
3. Refer to the page instructions for how to cut each appliqué. Sometimes you trace appliqués directly on the marked line, and sometimes you rough cut, leaving 2" all around the marked line. Be sure to trace the dashed lines on the shooting star flare onto the top layer of fabric.

   Appliqués for the Kid's Cape:
   - *Shooting star:* For the star, cut 1 of each size: 1 main color, 1 accent color; for the flare, cut 2: 1 main color, 1 accent color.
   - *Lightning bolt:* Cut 1 of each size: 1 main color, 1 accent color.

   Appliqués for the Sidekick (Dog's) Cape:
   - *Shooting star:* For the star, cut 1 of each size: 1 main color, 1 accent color; for the flare, cut 2: 1 main color, 1 accent color.
   - *Lightning bolt:* Cut 1 of each size: 1 main color, 1 accent color, or from lining fabric.

   Appliqués for the Hat (use the same patterns as for the Sidekick's Cape):
   - *Shooting star:* For the star, cut 1 of each size: 1 main color, 1 accent color; for the flare, cut 2: 1 main color, 1 accent color.
   - *Lightning bolt:* Cut 1 of each size: 1 main color, 1 accent color.

   If you're using woven fabrics instead of felt for the Hat appliqués, be sure to cut one of each piece and then flip the pattern to cut the others so you have mirror images.
4. Proceed to the sewing instructions for each item.

kid's cape

Shooting star appliqué

1. Trace around the templates with the water-soluble pen directly on the felt. Cut out the shapes, leaving extra fabric around the two flares. You can cut the stars directly on the traced outlines (see A).
2. Center the smaller star over the larger one. Pin or fuse it in place, and then topstitch the layers together.
3. Layer the flare pieces. Using a water-soluble fabric pen, trace the dashed lines from the flare template onto the top layer. Pin the two pieces together and stitch along the dashed lines and then around the outside edges.
4. Trim close to the stitching around the outside edges.
5. Using the reverse appliqué technique (see page 25), cut out the center portion of the flare, close to the stitching, to reveal the lower layer (see B).
6. Position the star over the flare as shown, with the star overlapping the flare by ¼" (6.4 mm). Baste or pin the star to the flare (see C).
7. Pin the star and flare in the center of the right side of the cape (see D). Topstitch them in place and around all edges of the larger star.
8. Proceed to the instructions for sewing the cape (see page 39).

Tip

Baste or fuse appliqués in place if you find it easier to secure them before topstitching. Pinning usually works for small appliqués.

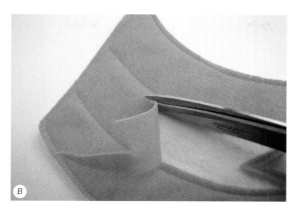

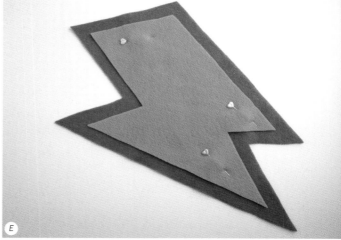

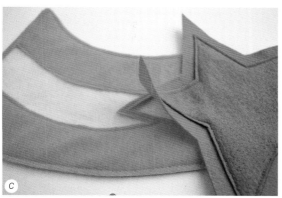

Lightning bolt appliqué

1. Pin the templates on the felt or trace around them with the water-soluble marker. Cut out the shapes directly on the marked outlines.
2. Center the smaller bolt over the larger one. Pin and then topstitch them together *(see E)*.
3. Place the bolt in center of the right side of the cape. Topstitch the appliqué to the cape *(see F)*.
4. Proceed to the instructions for sewing the cape (see page 39).

Tip

Before sewing the cape fabric and lining together, you might want to fuse small pieces of fusible interfacing on the wrong side, directly behind the hook-and-loop tape. This will add strength and some stability to the neck closing.

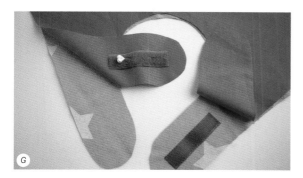

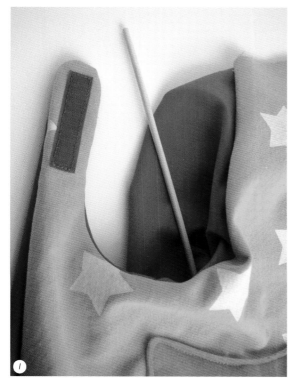

Making the cape

1. Pin the hook-and-loop tape to the neckline tab. Pin the softer (loop) side on the right side of the lining, and the rough (hook) side on the right side of the cape top. Stitch around the edges of the tape twice to give it extra strength (see G).
2. Pin the cape top and lining with the right sides together.
3. Sew around the cape, leaving an 8" (20.3 cm) opening on one side of cape (as marked on the pattern).
4. Trim the raw edges to ¼" (6.4 mm) (use pinking shears if you have them). Do **not** trim the opening; leave those edges untrimmed (see H).

5. Turn the cape right side out through the opening. Carefully use a point turner or chopstick to help push out both neckline tabs (see I).
6. Press the stitched edges of the cape. Turn the raw edges of the opening inward. Do **not** iron over the hook-and-loop tape (it will melt).
7. Topstitch around the edges of the cape, closing the opening as you stitch (see J).

sidekick cape

✎ **EASY**

Help your best friend and sidekick
be super, too!

1. Center a lightning bolt appliqué or a shooting star appliqué in the center of the cape fabric. You can even cut an appliqué piece from the lining fabric and position it under the felt appliqué if Fido wants a double-duty appliqué!

2. Fuse or topstitch the appliqué in place. If you topstitch, use a slightly longer, 3" (7.6 cm)-long stitch, ⅛" (3.2 mm) from the cut edge (see A).

3. Pin the cape and lining with the right sides together and stitch around the outside edge, leaving the opening for turning as marked on the template. Trim the seam allowances except for at the opening.

4. Turn the cape right side out through the opening (see B).

5. Use the point turner or chopstick to smooth the edges and form nice corners. Press the cape and press the edges of the opening to the inside. Topstitch around the entire cape, closing the opening as you stitch.

6. Press the top of the cape toward the lining at the foldline as shown. Stitch the top edge of the cape in place to create a channel for the dog collar (see C).

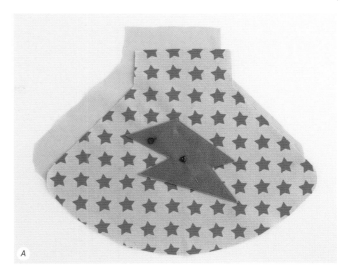

A

B

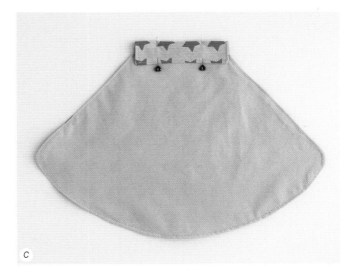

C

Tips

• So you don't have to remove the dog's collar to attach the cape, you can add a set of ¾" (2 cm)-long buttonholes within the collar channel.

• To keep the cape from spinning when your sidekick goes for a run, tack a piece of twill tape to each side of the cape, so you can tie the cape in place. You'll need to try the cape on your dog to find the best location for the ties.

mask

This simple tie-on mask is a great alternative (or addition) to the Superhero Hat (see page 44). It's made with felt—which isn't woven and has no grain, so the cut edges won't fray—so there's no need to sew. And, it's reversible!

Actually, there are a few ways you can make this mask: (1) you can just use iron-on adhesive and go completely no-sew; (2) you can use the iron-on adhesive and add topstitching; or (3) you can skip the iron-on adhesive and sew the pieces together. The instructions will help you with all the options.

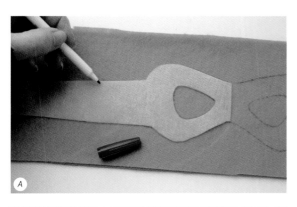

A

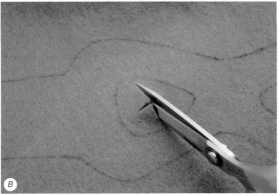

B

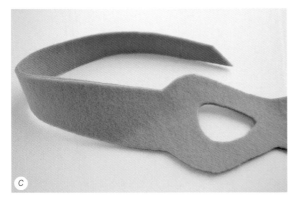

C

1. Cut the felt and the iron-on adhesive into 35" x 4" (89 x 10.2 cm) strips; two of felt and one adhesive. (Don't cut a strip of adhesive if you plan to only stitch the mask pieces together.)

2. Trace around the mask template with a water-soluble fabric pen directly on one strip of felt, but the template needs to be flipped. Trace the first half and then flip the template along the centerline to trace the rest of the mask. This is called a mirror image. *(see A)*.
   Note: Skip step 3 if you intend to sew the mask layers together without adhesive.

3. Following the manufacturer's instructions, use the iron-on adhesive to fuse the two strips of felt together. Make sure that the mask tracing is visible and the heat setting on the iron is no higher than medium.

4. To make the eyeholes, clip an X inside the eye area before trimming along the marked eyehole cutting lines *(see B)*.

5. **For a total no-sew option:** Simply cut around the entire mask along the traced lines *(see C)*.

6. **To add topstitching around the mask:** Stitch over the traced lines (including the eyeholes), then cut out the mask a scant ⅛" (3.2 mm) from the stitching *(see D)*.

D

superhero hat

This super-cute and super-powerful hat is a great accessory to the all-powerful cape. Choose your favorite appliqué—or use a different one on each side—and feel the power!

Tip

Use a fun color thread for topstitching around the edge of the hat!

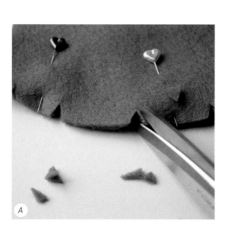

A

B

C

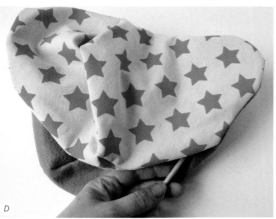

D

E

F

Making the hat

1. Cut little triangles in the seam allowance of the gusset and the side hat pieces so it's easier to sew the curved seams. Repeat with lining pieces. Pin the side hat pieces to each side of the gusset with right sides together for both the lining and the outside of the hat. Be sure edges and notches align (see A).

2. Sew the seams and then trim the seam allowances to ¼" (6.4 mm). Use pinking shears if you have them (see B).

3. Finger-press the seams toward the sides of the hat. Pin the outside hat and the lining with right sides together so the seams and cut edges align (see C).

4. Stitch around the edge of the hat, leaving the center bottom edge unstitched. Backstitch at the beginning and end of the seam. Trim the seam allowances except for the opening; leave those edges untrimmed. Turn the hat right side out (see D).

5. Carefully press the outer edges of the hat. Turn the raw edges of the opening inward and pin the opening closed (see E).

6. Topstitch around the edges of the hat, closing the opening as you stitch (see F).

Making and attaching the lightning bolt appliqué

Be sure to make two appliqués, following the instructions below for each one. Or make one shooting star (see opposite) and one lightning bolt and feel free to mix up different color felts.

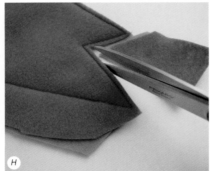

1. Trace around the templates with the water-soluble marker. You'll need three lightning bolts for each appliqué and at least one lightning bolt should be a different color from the other two. Don't trace the dashed lines that fill the center of the template yet. Rough cut out the shapes, leaving extra felt around all the markings. Pin three felt layers together, with the darker color on top (see G).

2. Topstitch the layers together, along the outside markings. Trim the extra fabric a scant ⅛" (3.2 mm) away from the stitching (see H).

3. Using the reverse appliqué technique (see page 25), cut out the center portion of the lightning bolt from the top layer, to reveal the layer beneath. This creates a felt border around the lightning bolt (see I).

4. Place the template over the appliqué and trace the dashed lines (or create your own pattern of lines) onto the lighter color felt that shows through the trimmed top layer. Cut a small opening through the bottom layer of felt and use a point turner or chopstick to insert fiberfill evenly around the lightning bolt (see J).

5. Smooth out the fiberfill and then stitch over the marked lines within the lightning bolt (see K).

6. Position the lightning bolts on each side of the hat, as shown so that the top points extend beyond the top of the hat. Edgestitch the appliqués in place, except the top points that extend off the hat (see L).

Making and attaching the shooting star appliqué

Be sure to make two appliqués, one for each one side of the hat. Or only make one if you prefer—superheroes don't need symmetry!

1. Trace around the templates with the water-soluble pen directly on the felt. You'll need two different color stars and three flares (at least one a different color from the other two) for each appliqué. When cutting out the stars, you can cut one smaller one and one larger one and layer them as shown or you can cut two larger stars and use the reverse appliqué technique described below and shown in the sample on page 44. Cut out the shapes, leaving extra fabric around the three flare pieces. You can cut the stars directly on the traced outlines.

2. Layer two stars together and topstitch twice around, close to the outside edge. If using the reverse appliqué technique (see page 25), cut out the center portion of the star from the top layer, close to the stitching, to reveal the layer beneath.

M

3. Layer the pieces for the shooting star's flare with the darker color felt on top of the remaining two layers. Using a water-soluble fabric pen, trace the dashed lines from the flare template onto the top layer. Pin the three pieces together and topstitch along the dashed lines and then around the outside edges.

4. Trim close to the stitching around the outside edges.

5. If using the reverse appliqué technique (see page 25), cut out the center portion of the flare from the top layer, close to the stitching, to reveal the layer beneath *(see M)*.

6. Pin the star over the flare so the star overlaps the flare by ¼" (6.4 mm) *(see N)*.

7. Position the star and flare together on one side of the hat, as shown on page 44, so the flare extends beyond the top of the hat. Pin and topstitch the appliqué in place.

8. Repeat to make and attach the second appliqué.

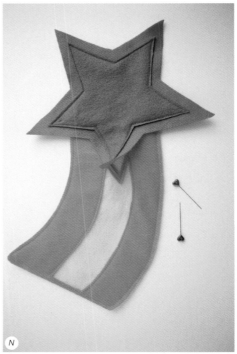

N

power cuffs

Nothing says superpower like power cuffs!
Use three different colors of felt for layers of color.

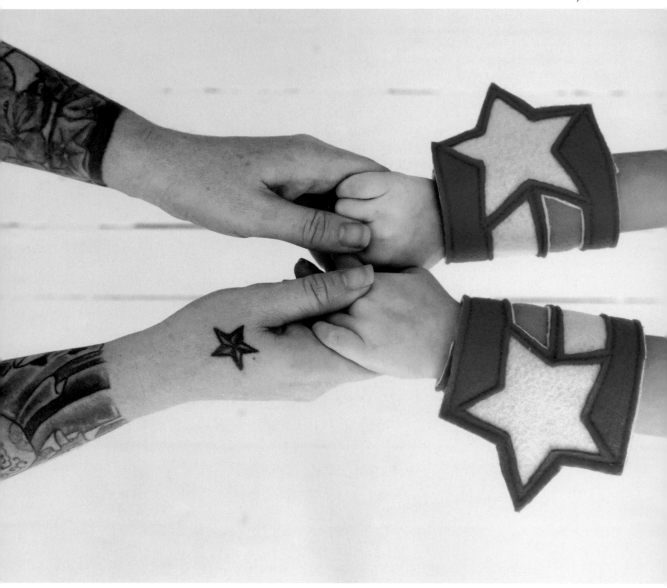

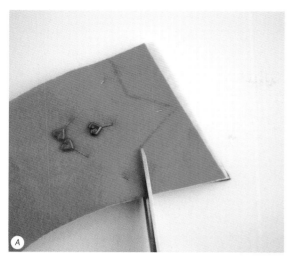

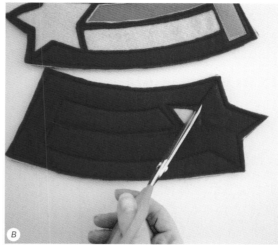

Shooting star cuffs

1. Layer three felt pieces with the lightest color in the center. Trace around the cuff template and cut out the three pieces. Flip the template over and cut the three remaining pieces. This will create mirror images so you have a right and left wrist cuff. Cut along the outside marked lines (see A).
2. Trace around the rest of the star and the interior lines indicated on the template.
3. Position the hook side of the hook-and-loop tape on the top layer along the straight edge. Stitch around the edge of the tape with matching thread two times.
4. Position the loop side of the hook-and-loop tape on the bottom layer so that it isn't visible from the right side and so it aligns with the hook side when the cuff closes. Try it on your child to determine the best location. Stitch around the edge three times, **but only through the bottom layer**.
5. Stitch all the layers together, ⅛" (3.2 mm) from the outer edge of the cuff. Also stitch the rest of the star and along the interior marked lines.
6. Using the reverse appliqué technique (see page 25), cut away the top layer of felt just inside the star stitching, revealing the middle layer of felt. Do the same for the two inside sections of the flare. Then choose one section of the flare and cut away the middle layer of felt to reveal the bottom layer of felt (see B).

Tip

As much as we all love the look of and memories in vintage sewing supplies, resist the urge to stitch together your super creations with any hand-me-down thread. These tend to become brittle over time, and with how hard your superhero will play in his or her new outfit, the seams will not hold up as well. By using new thread, you'll maximize years of fun and play!

Lighting bolt cuffs

1. Layer three felt pieces. Trace around the cuff template and cut out the three pieces. Flip the template over and cut the three remaining pieces. This will create mirror images so you have a right and left wrist cuff. Cut along the outside marked lines.

2. Position the loop side of the hook-and-loop tape on the bottom layer, near the shaped edge so that it isn't visible from the right side and so it aligns with the hook side when the cuff is closed. Try it on your child to determine the best location. Stitch around the edge three times, **but only through the bottom layer**.

3. Stitch all the layers together ⅛" (3.2 mm) from the outer edge of the cuff and over the inside traced marking for the lightning bolt. Clip a small opening through the top layer of felt in the center of the traced lightning bolt *(see C)*.

4. Carefully cut away the top layer of felt, just inside the lightning bolt stitching to reveal the middle layer of felt using the reverse appliqué technique (see page 25) *(see D)*.

5. Position the hook side of the hook-and-loop tape on the top layer along the straight edge of the cuff. Stitch around the edge of the tape with matching thread two times, through all layers *(see E)*.

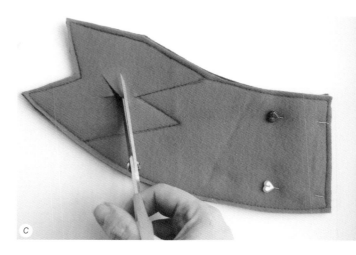

C

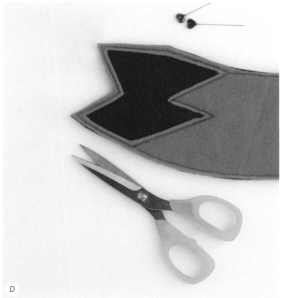

D

E

pirates

Arrrgh, matey! It's time to sail
away in search of buried
treasure and then, of course,
be back in time for dinner!
Just imagine: With an eye
patch and pirate hat, your kids
will rule the seven seas!

getting ready to sew

It's all about the accessories! And, the simple shapes of the skull, crossbones, and star (or heart) are very easy to cut out and apply. So go ahead and make a banner to match the capes! And don't forget to make a grand supply of very cool hats with a vast assortment of pirate medals.

You can make a marching banner by creating a casing for a rod up the back of it, or run a dowel through the top edge so you can hang it wherever your pirates want to plunder. I keep our pirate banner in the entrance to my studio, hanging just as you see it, in our bathtub sailboat!

Instructions are provided for a pirate cape, an eye patch, a hat with an assortment of medallion appliqués, a banner, and a skull and crossbones appliqué.

WHAT YOU'LL NEED

Basic tool kit (see page 12)

Templates (see Patterns and Measurements, right)

FABRICS AND NOTIONS

Fabric suggestions: broadcloth, quilting cottons, cotton canvas, denim, chambray, ticking, felt (for the appliqués)

For the cape:

1 yard (0.9 m) of 45" (1.14 m) wide fabric for the right side of the cape

1 yard (0.9 m) of 45" (1.14 m) wide fabric for the lining

3" (7.6 cm) of ½" (1.3 cm) wide Velcro/hook-and-loop tape

For the cape appliqué:

½ yard (0.5 m) of white felt for each appliqué

Remnant of red felt for the heart

Remnant of gold felt for the star

For the eye patch:

2 pieces of 4" x 5" (10.2 cm x 12.7 cm) remnants of fabric or felt

Package of ½" (1.3 cm) wide, fold-over elastic in black (or a color or pattern of your choice)

For the hat:

2 pieces of fabric, each 15" x 20" (38.1 cm x 50.8 cm)

felt remnants for the medallion appliqués

For the banner:

24" x 30" (61 cm x 76.2 cm) piece of felt or heavyweight fabric for the banner

½ yard (0.5 m) felt for the appliqué, two colors

½" (1.3 cm) diameter wooden dowel, 24" (61 cm) long

Twine to hang the banner (optional)

PATTERNS AND MEASUREMENTS

Trace the pattern pieces for all the projects you intend to make, including the appliqués, onto tracing paper or lightweight cardboard according to the instructions on page 24. Be sure to copy any pattern markings, such as notches and placement indicators, onto the templates. Cut out the traced patterns to make reusable templates.

PATTERNS ARE PROVIDED FOR THE FOLLOWING ITEMS:

Cape (pattern sheet 1)

Eye patch (page 123)

Appliqués (pages 121, 123, 131, and pattern sheet 1)

MEASUREMENTS ARE PROVIDED FOR THE FOLLOWING ITEMS:

Hat

Banner

Tracing the patterns and cutting the fabrics

1. The cape template will need to be placed on the fabric fold (see pages 19 and 20). Cut one cape from fabric and one from lining.
2. The hat and banner are cut from measurements. You can use the water-soluble fabric pen to mark the measurements before cutting. Cut the fabrics along the markings, two hat fabrics for each hat and one banner from felt. Shape the bottom of the banner—or don't—whatever you wish! Cut the following from measurements:
   • *For hat:* Cut two different pieces of fabric, each 15" x 20" (38 x 50 cm) for each hat
   • *For banner:* Cut one piece of fabric 24" x 30" (61 x 76 cm)
3. Trace around the eye patch and all appliqué templates directly on the fabric with a water-soluble fabric pen. Choose either the star or heart for the top of the skull and crossbones appliqué. Add the white circles to top the crossbones, if you wish. Cut out the eye patch and appliqué pieces directly on the marked lines.
   • *Large star:* Cut 1 for cape appliqué
   • *Large heart:* Cut 1 for cape appliqué and 1 for banner appliqué
   • *Skull:* Cut 1 for cape appliqué and 1 for banner appliqué
   • *Crossbones:* Cut 2 for cape appliqué and 2 for banner appliqué
   • *Small circle for over crossbones (optional):* Cut 2 for cape appliqué and 2 for banner appliqué
   • *Assortment of medallion shapes* for hats

   For crossbones and small circle over crossbones:
   If you're using woven fabrics instead of felt, be sure to cut 1 of each piece and then flip the pattern to cut the other so you have the mirror images.
4. Proceed to the sewing instructions for each item.

Tip

If you want to make the banner from woven cloth, you can hem the edges or leave them raw so they can ravel.

skull and crossbones cape

EASY

Tip

Pin or spray adhesive the felt appliqué pieces to hold them to the cape top to make stitching easier.

1. Pin (or fuse) all the pieces for the skull and crossbones appliqué on the right side of the cape fabric—center as shown. Use either the star or heart to top off the appliqué and add or eliminate the two circles at the top of the crossbones. Your choice!
2. Topstitch (or hand whipstitch) around all the cut edges to secure the appliqués (see A).
3. Follow steps 1 to 7 for making the Superhero Kid's Cape on pages 36 to 39.

banner

 EASY

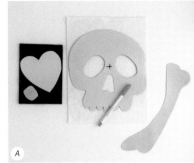

A

B

1. Trace around the appliqué templates with the water-soluble pen directly on the felt. Cut out the appliqué pieces on the marked lines. Be sure to add the white circles over the crossbones (see A).
2. Cut out the flag according to the dimensions provided and then shape the lower edge as desired.
3. Pin or fuse the appliqué pieces onto the center of the flag. Topstitch (or just fuse) around all the cut appliqué edges (see B).
4. Fold the top edge of the flag to the wrong side and edgestitch the cut edge in place to create a channel opening for the dowel. Slide the dowel through the opening.
5. To hang the banner, tie a length of twine to each end of the dowel.

Tips

- Blanket stitch, with embroidery floss for extra emphasis, the appliqués in place (see page 26).

- If you want to hang the flag on a vertical pole as shown above, simply stitch a piece of felt about 1½" (3.8 cm) wide by the length of the flag to the center of the back of the flag. Be sure to stitch the sides and across the top of the felt casing, but leave it open at the bottom. Attach the casing before the appliqué.

- Get creative and add a pennant and some scary blackbirds!

pirate hat

This is another great no-sew option. Simply cut the same two pieces of fabric and just use iron-on adhesive to fuse them with the wrong sides together. The edges might fray a bit, but it seems unlikely that unruly edges would bother a pirate! Follow all the same steps as for a sewn hat.

A

B

C

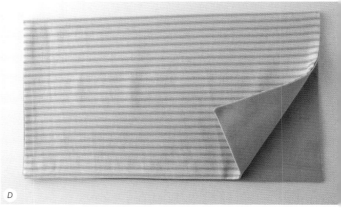

D

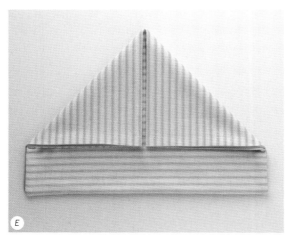

E

1. Trace around a variety of small medallion templates with the water-soluble pen directly on colorful pieces of felt. Or, draw your own shapes directly on the felt *(see A)*.
2. Cut each hat fabric 15" x 20" (38.1 cm x 50.8 cm).
3. Pin the two hat fabrics with right sides together and stitch around the perimeter, leaving an opening for turning the fabrics right side out *(see B)*.
4. Turn the fabrics right side out through the opening, gently using a point turner or chopstick to help push out the corners *(see C)*.
5. Carefully press the outer edges of the hat with an iron. Turn the raw edges of the opening inward. Topstitch around the edges of the hat, closing the opening as you stitch, or hand-stitch the opening closed.
6. Fold the fabric in half horizontally so that the fabric you want to form the point is on the outside and the fabric you want to form the bottom band is on the inside *(see D)*.
7. Fold the top corners down so they meet in the center, as shown. Press *(see E)*.

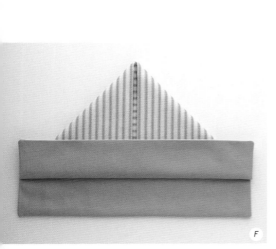

F

G

H

I

8. To create the brim, on the front of the hat, fold the bottom of the fabric up, about 2½" (6.4 cm) to form the bottom band, as shown *(see F)*.

9. Layer the appliqué shapes. Add tails as desired *(see G)*.

10. Either glue or stitch the various shapes together to create the medallions *(see H)*.

11. Topstitch the medallions onto the front of the hat through the top two fabric layers. Be careful that you don't stitch the back and front of the hat together! Don't stitch the tails; they'll fall over the bottom band.

12. At the back of the hat, fold the bottom of the fabric up onto the hat, about 2½" (6.4 cm), so it matches the width of the front band. Pin and topstitch the outside edges of the bands together to help the hat retain its shape *(see I)*.

eye patch

Get creative and decorate your eye patch with a fun appliqué.

A

1. Trace around the eye patch template onto two fabrics and transfer the elastic placement markings onto the wrong side of both fabrics. Trace around the small heart appliqué template on a piece of felt (see A).

Tip

For an authentic touch, use a woven fabric that frays easily for one of the eye patch layers so you can unravel the edge a bit!

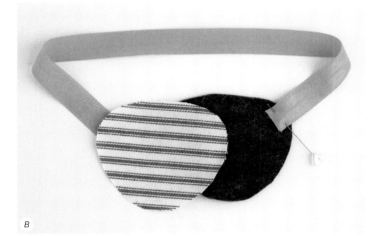

B

2. Pin the ends of the elastic to the wrong side of one eye patch at the markings so the ends will be sandwiched between the two layers. Make sure the elastic isn't twisted. Stitch the ends in place (see B).

3. Layer the eye patch pieces with wrong sides together and the elastic ends between them and topstitch around the eye patch.

4. You can glue or topstitch a small heart (or any of the medallion shapes) in the center of the eye patch. If you used a woven fabric as one of the eye patch layers, you can use your fingers to fray the edge for a more ragged look (see C).

C

fairy queen and dragon king

Whether your fairy queen and dragon king are off to protect their loyal subjects or make wishes come true, anything is possible with their very own hand-painted wings and crowns.

getting ready to sew

It's good to be queen and king, especially when you get to paint your own wings and crowns! The shoulder straps make it easy to adjust the wings for comfort and better fit and the fairy crown ties in place so it fits everyone—even the dowager queen mother! The dragon king's crown adjusts for fit with hook-and-loop tape.

Painting (see page 78) is the perfect way to let your child's imagination take wing! If you make the wings and crowns in plain canvas, they become a canvas for your king and queen to paint! Beware! You might have to make several sets for your royal artists!

Instructions are provided for fairy wings, crowns, and a star scepter.

WHAT YOU'LL NEED

Basic tool kit (see page 12)

Templates (see Patterns, right)

If you're planning to paint your projects, see page 78 for details.

FABRICS AND NOTIONS

Fabric suggestions: neutral color, lightweight cotton canvas or heavyweight muslin (7-ounce [200 g] cotton duck cloth was used to make the samples)

For the wings:

½ yard (0.5 m) of 45" (1.14 m) wide fabric for each set of wings

60" of 1" (2.5 cm) wide twill tape for each set of wings

½ yard (0.5 m) of batting for each set of wings

For the fairy queen crown:

¼ yard (23 cm) of 45" (1.14 m) wide fabric

½ yard (0.5 m) of 1" (2.5 cm) wide twill tape

For the dragon king crown:

¼ yard (23 cm) of 45" (1.14 m) wide fabric

3" (7.6 cm) of hook-and-loop tape or ribbon

For the scepter:

Remnant of felt for the star

Dowel, ½" (1 cm) diameter, 25" (64 cm) long

½ yard (0.5 m) lengths of assorted colorful ribbons

Tip

Although kids love to paint, these crowns and wings could be made in patterned fabrics or even fabrics flecked with gold and silver. You can also glue gemstones or attach nailheads or grommets for quick embellishments.

PATTERNS

Trace the pattern pieces for all the projects you intend to make, including the appliqués, onto tracing paper or lightweight cardboard according to the instructions on page 24. Be sure to copy any pattern markings, such as notches and placement indicators, onto the paper templates. Cut out the traced patterns to make reusable templates.

PATTERNS ARE PROVIDED FOR THE FOLLOWING ITEMS:

Fairy Queen Wing (pattern sheet 1)

Dragon King Wing (pattern sheet 1)

Fairy Queen Crown (patern sheet 2)

Dragon King Crown (pattern sheet 2)

Any star appliqué in the back of this book

Tracing the patterns and cutting the fabrics

1. Lay out the following templates and cut out the fabric as indicated.
   - *Fairy queen wing (front):* Cut 1 on the fabric fold; place dotted line on the fabric fold
   - *Fairy queen wing (back):* Cut 1, then flip the template and cut 1
   - *Dragon king wing (front):* Cut 1 on the fabric fold; place dotted line on the fabric fold
   - *Dragon king wing (back):* Cut 1, then flip the template and cut 1
   - *Fairy queen crown:* Cut 2
   - *Dragon king crown:* Cut 2; measure your child's head and add to the circumference of the pattern as needed and as indicated on the pattern.
2. Trace the star template directly on the felt two times and cut out the star directly on the marked lines.

Tip

For the back of the wings, if you are using canvas or felt with no wrong or right side, you can simply cut 2 at the same time.

fairy queen crown

🧵 **EASY**

1. Use the crown pattern to cut two crown pieces. Use the dotted line at the bottom edge as the cutting line.
2. Cut the twill tape into two 18" (45.7 cm)-long pieces for the straps.
3. With cut edges together, stitch a piece of twill tape to the right side of one crown piece 1" (2.5 cm) up from the bottom edge at each side. With the tie ends sandwiched between them and right sides together, pin the two crown pieces across the top points and side edges (see A).
4. Stitch up one side, across the pointed top edge, and down the other side. Leave the bottom edge open. Use pinking shears to trim the seam allowance and clip into the seam allowance at the inside V's.
5. Turn the crown right side out and use the point turner to poke out the corners and points. Extend the tie ends out. Press the crown and press the seam allowances at the bottom edge to the inside (see B).
6. Topstitch the bottom edge to close up the crown (see C).
7. The finished crown fastens as shown (see D). Now it's time to paint (see page 78)!

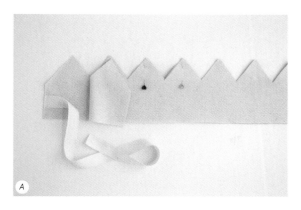

A

B

C

D

Tip

When stitching a jagged edge, sometimes it's easier to take one or two horizontal stitches between the points. This creates more of a U shape than a V shape between the points.
Your choice!

dragon king crown

EASY

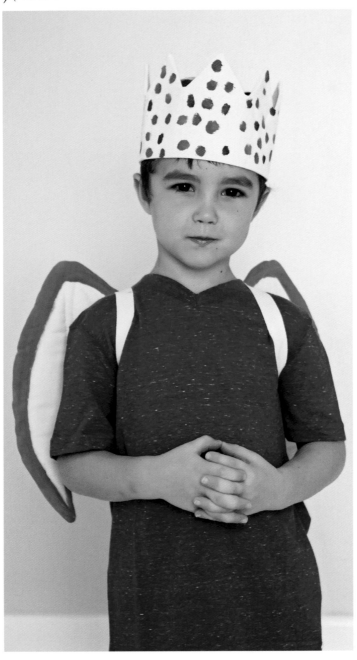

1. Use the crown template to cut two crown pieces. Copy the placement marking for the hook and loop tape onto the fabric with the fabric-marking pen. Use the solid line at the straight bottom edge for the cutting line.

2. With right sides together, pin the two crown pieces across the top points and side edges.

3. Stitch up one side, across the pointed top edge, and down the other side. Leave the bottom edge open. Use pinking shears to trim the seam allowance and clip into (see page 73) the seam allowance at the inside V's.

4. Turn the crown right side out and use the point turner to poke out the corners and points. Press the crown and press the seam allowances at the bottom edge to the inside.

5. Topstitch the bottom edge to close up the crown. Position the hook-and-loop tape as indicated on the pattern, so one piece is on the right side of the crown and the corresponding piece is on the inside of the crown. Make sure they line up and that the crown fits your child. Edgestitch the pieces in place.

6. Now it's time to paint (see page 78)!

wings

The instructions are the same for both the Fairy Queen and Dragon King wings, but the step photographs show the Fairy Queen wings.

/M INTERMEDIATE

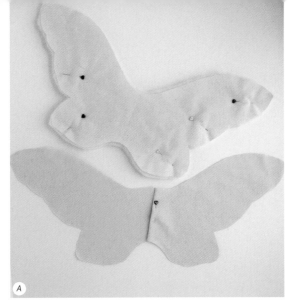

A

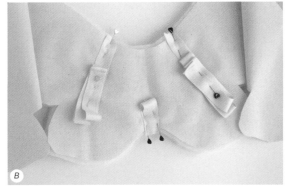

B

C

D

1. For the front wings and batting, position the dotted line on the fabric fold, to cut one fabric piece and one batting piece. Use the same template to cut two fabric pieces for the back wings. Copy the placement marking for the straps onto the right side of front fabric piece with the water-soluble fabric pen.

2. Position the wrong side of the front fabric wings over the batting.

3. Fold and press the center edge of one of the back wing fabric pieces ½" (1.3 cm) to the wrong side and overlap it over the opposite back wing piece. Pin (see A).

4. Cut one piece of twill tape for the bottom loop 4" (10.2 cm) long. Cut the remainder of the twill tape in half for the straps.

5. Pin the twill tape to the right side of the front wings at the placement markings with the cut edges aligned. Fold up the long pieces of the twill tape so they don't get caught in the stitching. Pin the loops as shown (see B).

6. Position the back wings over the right side of the front wings as shown. The piece with the pressed center edge should be on the bottom and the remaining back piece should cover the folded edge (see C).

7. Stitch all around the perimeter of the wings. Trim the seam allowances and, in particular, trim the batting close to the stitching. Remove any pins still holding the straps.

8. Turn the wings right side out through the opening in the center back of the wings. Extend the bottom loop and straps.

9. Stitch along the folded edge of the back opening to close up the wings. Topstitch around the edge of the wings and then as desired to create patterns inside the wings (see D).

10. Finish the cut edge of the straps so they don't ravel by folding the cut edge to one side and stitching it in place.

11. Now it's time to paint (see page 78)!

painting playwear

It's so easy to add animal markings, decorative designs, Fairy Queen glamour, and Dragon King details with fabric paint. And your kids will love to do it themselves!

Painting playwear details should be fun. Anything goes and nothing is a mistake. A few general tips make it easy.

WHAT YOU'LL NEED

Fabric paints in a variety of colors

Plastic plates for palettes

Craft paintbrush with fairly short and stiff bristles to help push the paint into the fabric fibers Container for water to rinse the brush when changing colors

Painting smocks

Paper towels for quick spills and to keep hands clean

Paper, fabric, or plastic dropcloth to protect your work surface

- *Dress for the mess.* Both you and your kids should wear old clothing.
- *Prewash the fabric (but not felt) to remove any sizing*, which may prevent the paint from adhering to the fabric. Press out any wrinkles, too.
- *Choosing the best paint is the hardest part.* You might want to try a few different fabric paints. It shouldn't be too thin or it will seep and spread, or too thick because it will be hard to spread. You also don't want the paint to stiffen the fabric once it's dry.
- *Dab minimal paint on the brush* and apply it with an up-and-down, dabbing motion.
- *Once the paint is dry*, your artists can paint the other side to make reversible crowns and wings.
- *You'll want to "set" the paints.* To make sure the paint is dry, wait at least 24 hours. Then throw the painted item in the dryer for about 20 minutes, or iron directly over the paint with a press cloth between the iron (set on medium heat with no steam) and the item for about 30 seconds (check the manufacturer's instructions on the paint bottle).

Tip

As an alternative to working with liquid paints, try fabric paint pens, or fabric paints in squeezable plastic bottles.

star scepter

Just get out your fabric glue and secure the ribbon ends inside one star with glue, insert the painted dowel, and then fuse or glue the two stars together.

1. Use the star template to cut two felt stars. Trim the ribbons into ½-yard (0.5 m) lengths.
2. Paint the dowel as desired. Let dry.
3. Pin one end of each of the ribbons on the inside of one star, near where the dowel will go. Tack the ribbon ends to the star.
4. Position the dowel in the center of the star, near the ribbons and so the top of the dowel is close to the top point of the star. Apply fabric glue to secure the dowel.
5. Position the remaining star over the first star so the ribbon ends and dowel are sandwiched between the two stars. Glue or topstitch the two stars together.

Tip

It might be easier to use spray paint to paint the dowel. Or, you can wrap it with colorful duct tape.

magicians

There's nothing up their sleeves! But with these twirly, swirly magical cloaks, they'll have tricks galore.

getting ready to sew

Abra-ca-da-bra! What child—or adult for that matter—doesn't wish for a little magic? All it takes is a cloak with a secret pocket and a special hat to make your magicians feel magical!

The ever-expanding scarf and simple rabbit add so much play-factor to this simple playwear set. Gather toys and stuffed animals from your own toy chest to add to the show!

Instructions are provided for a magician cloak, hat, rabbit, and scarf, an assortment of appliqués, and, of course, a magic wand.

WHAT YOU'LL NEED

Basic tool kit (see page 12)

Templates (see Patterns and Measurements, right)

FABRICS AND NOTIONS

Fabric suggestions:

For the cape: mid-weight canvas, cotton broadcloth, felt

For the bunny: fleece, quilting cotton for the ears

For the hats: felt

For the scarf: cotton Kona

For the cloak:

1½ yards (1.4 m) of 45" (1.14 m) wide fabric for the right side of the cloak

1½ yards (1.4 m) of 45" (1.14 m) wide fabric for the lining and neck tie

Use colorful ribbon or twill tape in place of fabric for the neckties—no sewing needed!

6½" x 8" (16.5 cm x 20.3 cm) fabric remnant for inside pocket

8" x 13" (20.3 cm x 33 cm) fabric remnant for inside pocket

For the appliqués:

For the stars: ¼ yard (23 cm) of felt in two or three colors to match the lining color

For the hearts and diamonds: ¼ yard (23 cm) of dark blue felt

For the spades and clubs: ¼ yard (23 cm) of black felt

For the bunny:

¼ yard (23 cm) of white felt

¼ yard (23 cm) or remnant for inside ears

pink and gray felt remnants for the appliqués

polyester fiberfill

For the hat:

¾ yard (68.6 cm) of 45" (1.14 m) wide fabric for the hat

¾ yard (68.6 cm) of lightweight fusible interfacing

Felt remnants for the appliqués

For the scarf:

8" x 10" (20.3 cm x 25.4 cm) scraps of colorful, light-weight fabrics

Use lightweight fabrics for the scarf, like silky lining fabrics, so they fit inside the pocket and shimmer when your magician performs.

For the wand:

Wooden dowel, ½" (1.3 cm) diameter and 12" (30.5 cm) long

Painter's tape, washi tape, or masking tape

Black and white paint (or any paint colors you prefer)

Paintbrush

String (for drying the dowel), optional

PATTERNS AND MEASUREMENTS

Trace the pattern pieces for all the costume pieces that you intend to make, including the appliqués, onto tracing paper or lightweight cardboard according to the instructions on page 24. Be sure to copy any pattern markings, such as notches and placement indicators, onto the paper templates. Cut out the traced patterns to make reusable templates.

PATTERNS ARE PROVIDED FOR THE FOLLOWING ITEMS:

Cloak (pattern sheet 2)

Collar (page 127)

Hat brim (pattern sheet 2)

Hat top (pattern sheet 2)

Infinity Scarf (page 129)

Rabbit body (pattern sheet 2)

Rabbit ears (page 125)

Rabbit arms (page 125)

Appliqués for magician and rabbit (pages 125, 131, 133, and 135)

MEASUREMENTS ARE PROVIDED FOR THE FOLLOWING ITEMS:

Necktie

Small inside pocket

Large inside pocket

Hat crown

Tracing the patterns and cutting the fabrics

1. Trace around the appliqué templates with the water-soluble pen directly on the felt. Cut out the appliqué pieces directly on the marked lines. For the Rabbit appliqués, see step 4.
   - *Large star:* Cut 2 for cloak
   - *Medium star:* Cut 2 for cloak and 2 for hat
   - *Small star:* Cut 2 for cloak and 1 for hat
   - *Spade:* Cut 3 or 4 for cloak
   - *Heart:* Cut 3 or 4 for cloak
   - *Diamond:* Cut 3 or 4 for cloak
   - *Club:* Cut 3 or 4 for cloak
2. Pin the templates for the following pieces onto the fabric and then cut them out. Transfer all marks from the templates to the fabric with the water-soluble fabric pen.
   - *Cloak:* Cut 4 each from both the fabric and the lining
   - *Cape collar:* Cut 1 each from both the fabric and the lining. Note: To make a stand-up collar, fuse medium-weight interfacing to the wrong side of the fabric.
   - *Hat brim:* Cut 2 from fabric; cut 1 from interfacing
   - *Hat top:* Cut 1 from fabric; cut 1 from lining; cut 1 from interfacing
3. Use the measurements to cut necktie pieces, pockets, and crown pieces.
   - *Necktie:* 2" x 23" (5 cm x 58.4 cm); cut 2
   - *Small inside pocket:* 6½" x 8" (15.2 cm x 20.3 cm); cut 1
   - *Large inside pocket:* 8" x 13" (20.3 cm x 33 cm); cut 1
   - *Hat crown:* 7" x 23" (17.8 cm x 58.4 cm); cut 1 from fabric; cut 1 from lining; cut 1 from interfacing
4. For the Rabbit, trace around the nose, small heart, tail appliqué templates with the water-soluble pen directly on the felt. Cut out the appliqué pieces directly on the marked lines. Use the Rabbit templates to cut out the fleece fabric for the body, arms, and ears. Cut the ear linings from contrast fabric.
   - *Rabbit body:* Cut 2
   - *Rabbit ears:* Cut 2 from felt; cut 2 from contrast fabric for lining
   - *Rabbit arms*: Cut 4
   - *Rabbit nose:* Cut 1
   - *Rabbit tail:* Cut 1
   - *Rabbit heart:* Cut 1
5. Lightweight, colorful, and leftover fabrics are perfect for the never-ending scarf. Cotton Kona is a good choice. Cut about 15 pieces using the template and pinking scissors. The cut edges can be left unfinished.
6. Proceed to the sewing instructions for each item.

cloak and collar

/\/\/\ INTERMEDIATE

1. Sew together the four cloak pieces cut from the fabric (not the lining). With right sides facing, pin and stitch two straight edges together to make the center back of the cloak.

2. With right sides together and notch markings aligned, pin and stitch the two remaining pieces to each side of the cloak back (these are the shoulder seams). Notch then trim the seam allowances and press the seams.

3. Repeat steps 1 and 2 with the lining pieces. Staystitch around the neck edge of both the outside of the cloak and the lining.

4. Pin or fuse all the appliqués on the right side of the outside cloak fabric, about 2½" (6.4 cm) up from the bottom edge or over from the center front edge. Refer to the photograph on the left or place them wherever and however you wish.

5. Topstitch the appliqués to the right side of the cloak.

6. Make both pockets. Press the top edge ½" (1.3 mm) to the wrong side and then ½" (1.3 cm) again and stitch 1" (2.5 cm) from the top edge. Press the remaining edges ½" (1.3 cm) to the wrong side.

7. Pin the pockets to the right side of the lining so they're on each side and near the center front opening. Edgestitch the sides and bottom of the pockets in place *(see A)*.

8. Fold each necktie piece in half lengthwise with right sides together. Stitch across the bottom and up the side. Use a point turner or chopstick to turn the neckties right side out. Press the neckties. **Note:** Alternatively, you can use ribbons as the neckties and eliminate this step.

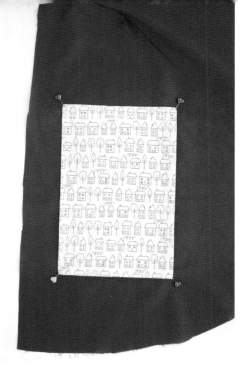

A

B

C

D

9. Pin the open end of one necktie ½" (1.3 cm) down from the top of the neck so the cut edges of the necktie and center front of the cloak align. Repeat on the opposite side with the remaining necktie. Pin the length of the necktie off to the side so it doesn't get caught in the stitching (in the next step).

10. Pin the collar fabric and collar lining pieces with right sides together and stitch the sides and outside edge. Leave the neck edge open. Trim the seam allowances and turn the collar right side out. Use the point turner or chopstick for neat corners, press the collar, and notch (see page 45) the neck edge.

11. Pin the lining side of the collar to the right side of the cloak along the neck edge matching markings. Baste the collar and neckties to the cloak (see B).

12. Pin the lining and cloak with right sides together and the collar and neckties sandwiched between them. Make sure the shoulder seams are aligned. Stitch around the entire cloak, leaving an opening for turning along the bottom edge (see C).

13. Trim the seam allowances, especially at the neck edge. Turn the cloak right side out. Press the seams and press the seam allowances at the opening to the inside. The collar and neckties extend out from the seam.

14. Topstitch around the edges of the cloak, closing the opening in the stitching (see D).

magician's hat

A

1. Following the manufacturer's instructions, fuse the interfacing to the wrong side of all the outer hat pieces: top, crown, brim.

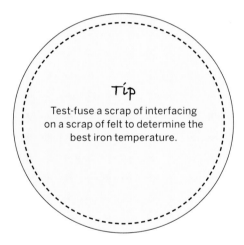

Tip

Test-fuse a scrap of interfacing on a scrap of felt to determine the best iron temperature.

2. Pin the star appliqués to right side of crown. (If your Magician is especially twinkly, cover the hat with stars!) If you wish, insert a bit of fiberfill behind each one. Topstitch the appliqués in place *(see A)*.
3. With right sides together, stitch the center back seam for crown. Repeat with the lining. Clip into the seam allowances on both open edges of the crown and on the top hat pieces.

4. Easing the fabrics to fit together smoothly, stitch the hat top to the crown with right sides together. Repeat with lining pieces. Finger-press the seams.
5. Clip into the seam allowance around the inner circumference of the brim. With right sides together, sew the bottom edge of the crown to the inside edge of the brim. Repeat with the remaining fabric brim and the crown lining.
6. With wrong sides together and the lining pieces tucked inside the fabric pieces, edgestitch the outside edges of the brims together. Trim the seam allowances. Tuck the lining inside the outside of the hat.

Tip

It's important to notch when sewing curved edges. This allows the fabric to stretch as you stitch. It's also good to divide the seam into quarters so you don't inadvertently stretch one of the pieces. Use a lot of pins!

never-ending scarf

NO-SEW

A

C

B

1. Pink the edges of all the various scarf pieces *(see A)*.
2. Knot them together at the acute corners to make an ever-expanding scarf *(see B)*.
3. Store the scarf in the inside pocket of the cape *(see C)*.

rabbit

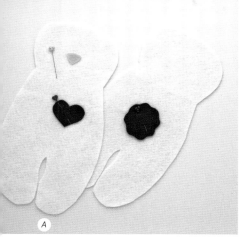

A

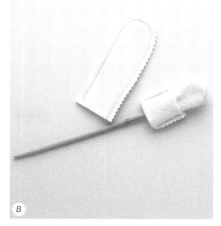

B

C

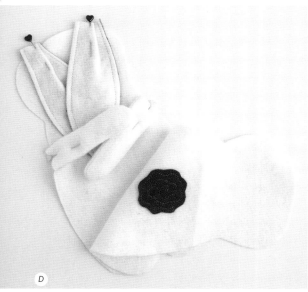

D

E

1. Position the heart and nose appliqués on one body and the tail on the other as shown. Topstitch them in place. Stitch a swirl pattern in the middle of the tail appliqué to add texture (see A).

2. Make the arms by sewing two arms together, leaving a narrow edge open for turning. If you have pinking shears, trim the seam allowances. Turn the arms right side out. Use a point turner or chopstick to smooth the edges. Finger-press the arms (see B)

3. Make the ears. Pin the ear and the ear lining right sides together. Stitch, leaving the bottom edge open for turning. Pink the edges and turn the ears right side out. Use the point turner or chopstick to smooth the seams and push out the point of the ear.

4. Stitch around the ears about ½" (1.3 cm) from the edge. Fold and pin a pleat at the bottom edge of each ear (as marked on the template) so that when the ears are attached to the bunny, the folds go toward the center (see C).

5. Lay out the front of the rabbit, right side up. Pin the arms in place as marked on the pattern. Pin the ears to the top of the head with the lining sides down and the pleat folds pointing toward the center. With the arms and ears pinned as shown, pin the back of the bunny, right side down to the rabbit front (see D).

6. Stitch around the rabbit, catching the ears and arms in the stitching. Leave an opening along the outside of one leg. Turn right side out.

7. Lightly stuff with the fiberfill. Turn the edges of the opening to the inside and hand-sew the opening closed (see E).

magic wand

1. Paint one end of the dowel with the white paint for approximately 4" (10.2 cm) from one end. Let the paint dry.
2. Carefully tape around both ends of the dowel, 3" (7.6 cm) from each end. Doing this masks the white section at the painted end and creates a clean paint line for the black paint at both ends.
3. Before painting the rest of the dowel, tie the string around the taped end of the dowel. Use the string to hang the dowel to avoid smudging the black paint.
4. Paint the untaped part of the dowel black. Let dry.
5. Paint the unpainted end with white paint (see A). Let dry.

woodland creatures

Just look how friendly
they are! This bunny and fox
could almost be siblings!

getting ready to sew

You can make these hats and tails in a variety of fabrics for a variety of animals. Create a whole menagerie!

The Superhero Hat and the hats in this chapter are made using very similar patterns, but a change in color and print makes for completely different looks, especially the Fox's Sherpa lining and the bold flannel print.

Instructions are provided for Bunny Hat, Bunny Powder Puff Tail, Fox Hat, Fox Tail, and a collection of appliqués for the Fox.

WHAT YOU'LL NEED

Basic tool kit (see page 12)

Templates (see Patterns and Measurements, right)

FABRICS AND NOTIONS

Fabric suggestions:

cotton, flannel, Sherpa fleece, felt (for the hats and appliqués)

For the bunny hat:

1 yard (0.9 m) of 45" (1.14 m) wide fabric for the right side of the hat and ears

½ yard (0.5 m) of 45" (1.14 m) wide Sherpa fleece for the lining

¼ yard (23 cm) of 45" (1.14 m) wide fabric for the neckties

¼ yard (23 cm) of 45" (1.14 m) wide fabric for the inside ears

For the bunny tail:

1 skein of yarn or purchased pompom

4" (10.2 cm) square of cardboard

For the fox hat and tail:

1 yard (0.9 m) of felt for the right side of the hat/tail and ear appliqué

½ yard (0.5 m) of 45" (1.14 m) wide flannel for the lining of the hat/tail and ears

¼ yard (23 cm) of white felt for the tail and appliqués

Polyester fiberfill for the tail

Black felt remnant for nose

PATTERNS AND MEASUREMENTS

Trace the pattern pieces for all the costume pieces that you intend to make, including the appliqués, onto tracing paper or lightweight cardboard according to the instructions on page 24. Be sure to copy any pattern markings, such as notches and placement indicators, onto the paper templates. Cut out the traced patterns to make reusable templates.

PATTERNS ARE PROVIDED FOR THE FOLLOWING ITEMS:

Hat gusset (pattern sheet 2)

Hat side (pattern sheet 2)

Fox ear (page 139)

Bunny hat ears/Fox tail (pattern sheet 2)

Appliqués (pages 137, 139, and pattern sheet 2)

MEASUREMENTS ARE PROVIDED FOR THE FOLLOWING ITEMS:

Bunny hat neckties

Fox tail tie ends

Tracing the patterns and cutting the fabrics

1. Trace around the appliqué templates with the water-soluble pen directly on the felt. Cut out the appliqué pieces directly on the marked lines. Transfer all markings from the templates to the fabric with the water-soluble fabric pen.
   - *Fox nose appliqué:* Cut 1
   - *Fox center bridge appliqué:* Cut 1 on fabric fold
   - *Fox side whisker:* Cut 2
   - *Fox hat ear tuft:* Cut 2
   - *Fox hat inner ear tuft:* Cut 2

2. Pin the following templates on the fabric and lining and cut out as indicated. Note that the shape for center front of the gusset is different for the Bunny and Fox. There are two gussets with different shaped center front cutting lines; the Bunny (same as the superhero) is gently curved inward and the Fox is shaped like a *V*.
   - *Hat gusset:* Cut 1 from fabric; cut 1 from lining
   - *Hat side:* Cut 2 from fabric; cut 2 from lining
   - *Fox hat ear:* Cut 2 from fabric; cut 2 from lining
   - *Bunny hat ears:* Cut 2 from fabric; cut 2 from lining;
   - *Fox tail:* Cut 1 from lining; cut 2 from different colors of felt

3. Cut two Bunny neckties, each 5" x 25" (12.7 cm x 63.5 cm). You might want to cut on the diagonal one narrow end of each necktie to match the shape shown in the photograph on page 107.

4. For the Fox tail tie ends, cut 1 strip of felt 1" x 16" (2.5 cm x 40.6 cm).

Proceed to the sewing instructions for each item.

Tip

You might want to shorten the ears on the Bunny Hat or the Fox's tail if your child isn't very tall! Simply remove a section from the top of the ear/tail pattern, as desired, on the "shorten here" dashed line.

bunny hat

INTERMEDIATE

Tip

For more information, refer to the step photographs for the Superhero Hat (page 44).

1. Make the ears as long as you would like; see the shortening lines on the pattern. Pin one ear and one lining piece with right sides together. Stitch around the ear, leaving the top edge open. Trim the seam allowance. Use the point turner to turn the ear right side out. Repeat to make the other ear. Press both ears. Fold the ears toward the lining as indicated on the pattern and pin (see A).

2. Make the neckties. Fold each necktie piece in half lengthwise with right sides together. Stitch across the bottom (shaped or straight) edge and up the open side. Leave the top edge open for turning. Trim the seam allowances. Turn the neckties right side out and press.

3. For the hat sides and gusset, cut notches in the seam allowance to make it easier to sew the curved seams. Pin the open edge of the neckties on the right side of each side hat piece at the marking, with raw edges aligned, as shown. Pin the rest of the necktie to the center of the hat so it doesn't get caught in the stitching (see B).

4. Pin one ear to the right side of one side hat at the placement marking, raw edges aligned so the fold in the ears is toward the back of the head and lining side

is down. Then pin the right side of the gusset over the side hat, aligning placement markings and sandwiching the ear between. Stitch the seams and then trim the seam allowances to ¼" (6.4 mm). Use pinking shears if you have them. Repeat with the remaining side hat and gusset. Finger-press the seams toward the sides of the hat (see C).

5. Pin and stitch the side hat lining pieces, one to each side of the gusset lining piece, matching the markings. Finger-press the seams toward the sides of the hat.

6. With right sides together, and the ears and neckties sandwiched between, stitch the outside hat and lining together all around the outside edge, leaving the seam open at the center back bottom edge.

7. Trim the seam allowances except for at the opening. Turn the hat right side out and extend the ears and neckties out. Turn the raw edges of the opening inward and hand-stitch the opening closed (see D).

bunny tail

This is super easy, no-sew, and a perfect project to share with your little bunny.

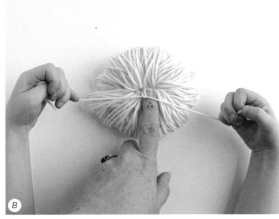

1. Wind the yarn around and around the 4" piece of cardboard until you have the desired thickness. I like a full, dense pompom (see A).
2. Cut a length of yarn about 18" (45.7 cm) long, or long enough to use as a tie belt. Slide the yarn off the cardboard and tie the length of yarn around the middle in a tight knot (see B).
3. With scissors, cut through the loops on both sides of the pompom.
4. Fluff the pompom and trim all the ends like you're giving it a little haircut, making sure you don't accidentally cut the tie ends! (See C.)
5. Use the tie ends in a belt loop or around your child's waist for a perfect bunny tail!

fox hat

$\wedge\wedge$ **INTERMEDIATE**

A

B

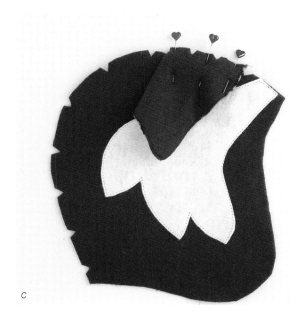

C

1. Layer a small inside ear tuft appliqué over a large inside ear tuft appliqué with bottom edges aligned; topstitch around all the edges. Then layer the large inside ear tuft appliqué over an ear lining piece and topstitch it in place. Repeat for the other ear *(see A)*.

2. For both ears, and with right sides together, stitch the appliquéd lining ear to the felt ear around all but the bottom edge. Turn the ears right side out. Finger-press the seams and then topstitch around all the edges. Fold the outside edge of both ears along the foldline to match the dots indicated on the pattern and as shown *(see B)*.

3. Cut notches in the seam allowance of the side hat and gusset to make it easier to sew the curved seams.

4. Position the side hat appliqués on the side hat pieces, as shown. Position the center bridge appliqué on the shaped end of the center hat, with the nose positioned over it, as shown. Topstitch all appliqués in place. Pin one folded ear to the right side of each side head, with the raw edges aligned and the lining side down *(see C)*.

5. Pin the side whisker seams to the gusset, matching markings, with the right sides together. Stitch the seams and then trim the seam allowances to ¼" (6.4 mm). Note: The center front of the gusset extends beyond the side hat pieces. Use pinking shears if you have them. Finger-press the seams toward the sides of the hat. Repeat this step with the side hat and center hat lining pieces.

6. With right sides together, and the ears sandwiched between, stitch the outside hat and lining together all around the outside edge, leaving the seam open at the center back bottom edge. The seams and markings should align.

7. Trim the seam allowances except for at the opening. Turn the hat right side out and extend the ears. Turn the raw edges of the opening inward and hand-stitch the opening closed.

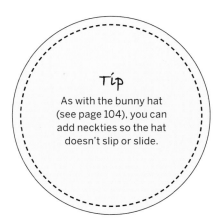

Tip
As with the bunny hat (see page 104), you can add neckties so the hat doesn't slip or slide.

fox tail

Are you a fennec fox, an arctic fox, or a swift fox? Play with color and pattern to find a fox that is your very own!

A

B

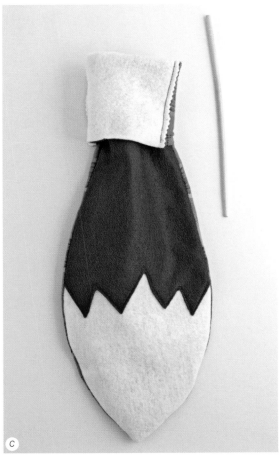

C

1. Cut a ragged, claw like edge about two-thirds of the way from the top of the tail on the darker color of felt for the tail, as shown *(see A)*.
2. Pin the claw-like felt tail over the whole felt tail and topstitch along the jagged edge of the top felt layer *(see B)*.
3. With right sides together, pin the appliquéd tail to the lining and stitch, leaving the top edge open for turning.
4. Turn the tail right side out and stuff the tail lightly with polyester fiberfill *(see C)*.
5. Fold the felt tie end strip in half and tuck the fold inside the top edge of the tail. Topstitch the tail closed, catching the tie end in the stitching so that the tie ends extend outward. Use the tie ends to secure the tail in a belt loop.

patterns

You'll find some of the patterns here and others in
the pocket in the front of the book. Use them to make
templates so that you can make these pieces
again and again.

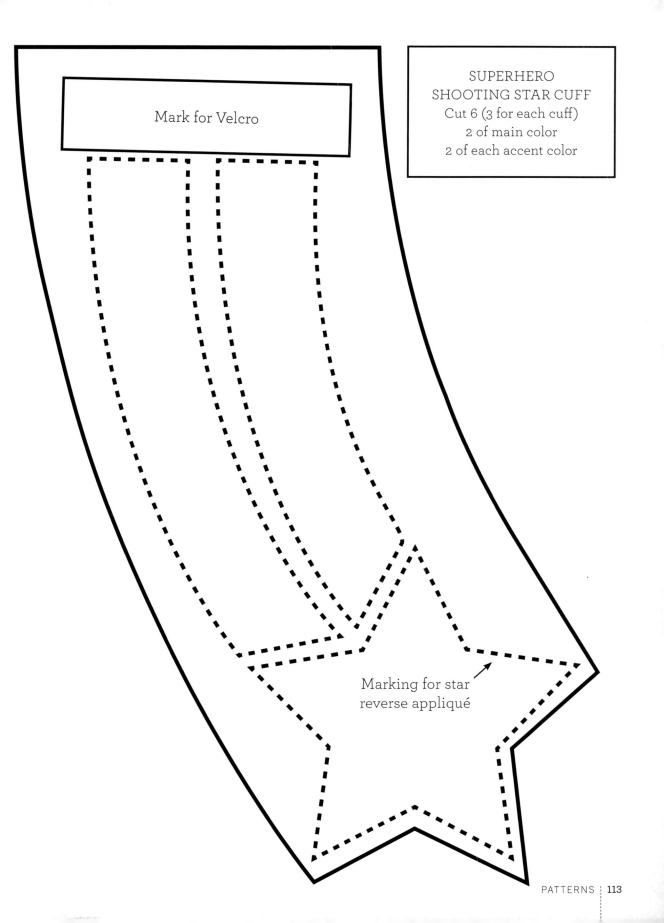

Mark for Velcro

SUPERHERO
SHOOTING STAR CUFF
Cut 6 (3 for each cuff)
2 of main color
2 of each accent color

Marking for star
reverse appliqué

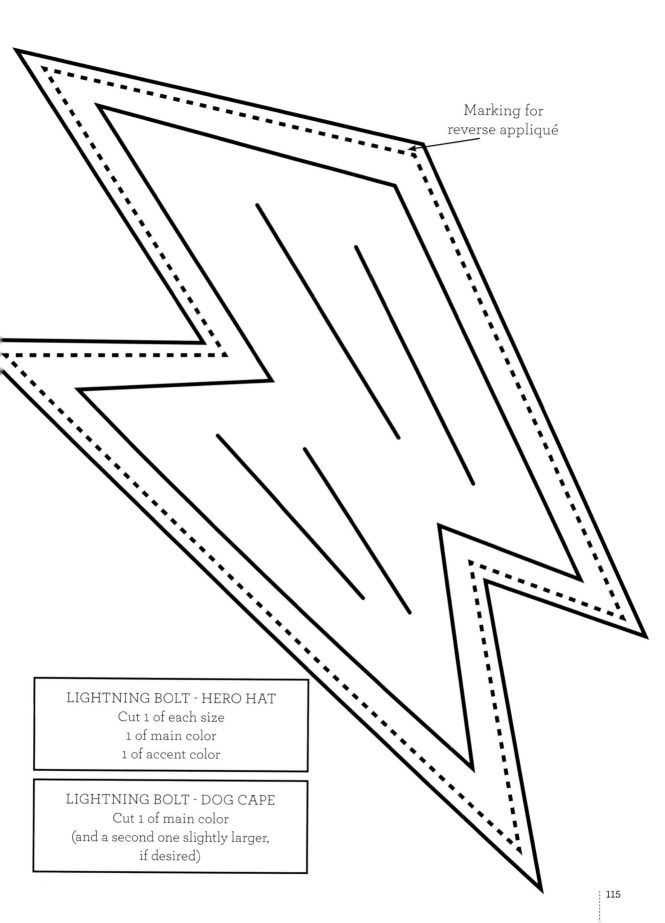

Marking for
reverse appliqué

LIGHTNING BOLT - HERO HAT
Cut 1 of each size
1 of main color
1 of accent color

LIGHTNING BOLT - DOG CAPE
Cut 1 of main color
(and a second one slightly larger,
if desired)

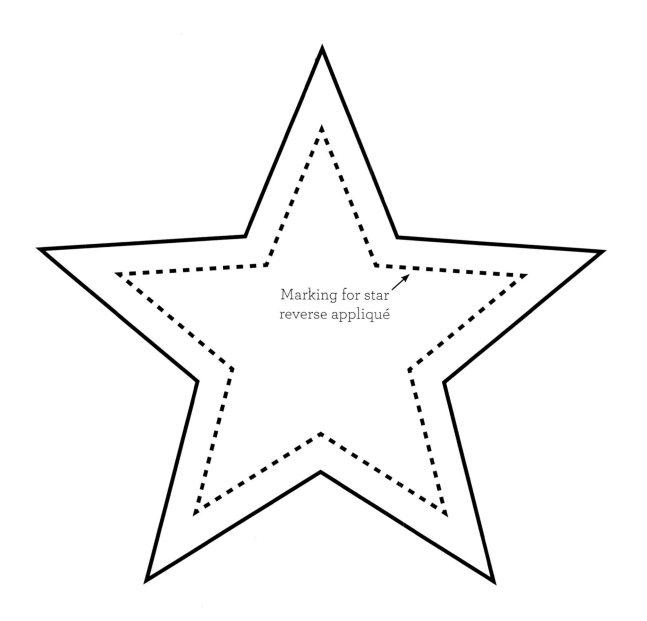

SHOOTING STAR - HERO HAT
Cut 2
1 of main color
1 of accent color

PIRATE CAPE - APPLIQUÉ
Cut 1

MAGICIAN CLOAK - APPLIQUÉ
Cut as needed

SHOOTING STAR -
DOG CAPE APPLIQUÉ
Cut 1 of each size
1 of main color
1 of accent color

Marking for star
reverse appliqué

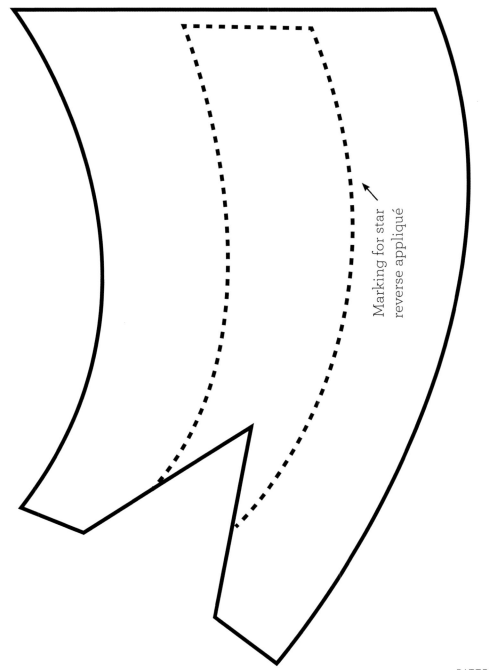

Marking for star
reverse appliqué

PIRATE - MEDALLIONS AND
EMBELLISHMENTS
Cut as needed

PIRATE - MEDALLIONS AND EMBELLISHMENTS

PIRATE EYE PATCH -
OPTIONAL EMBELLISHMENTS
Cut 1 - felt

Center elastic   Center elastic

PIRATE EYE PATCH
Cut 2

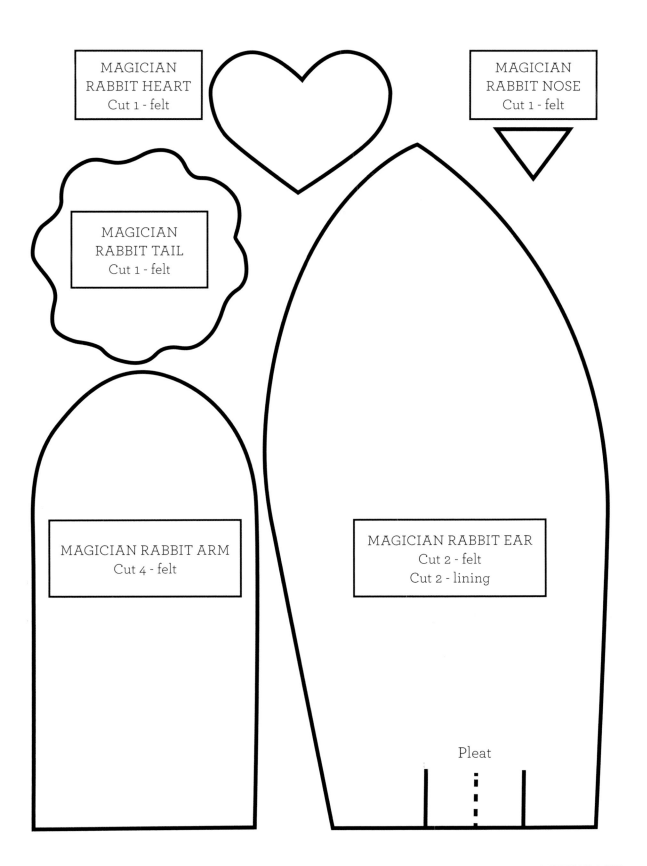

MAGICIAN
RABBIT HEART
Cut 1 - felt

MAGICIAN
RABBIT NOSE
Cut 1 - felt

MAGICIAN
RABBIT TAIL
Cut 1 - felt

MAGICIAN RABBIT ARM
Cut 4 - felt

MAGICIAN RABBIT EAR
Cut 2 - felt
Cut 2 - lining

Pleat

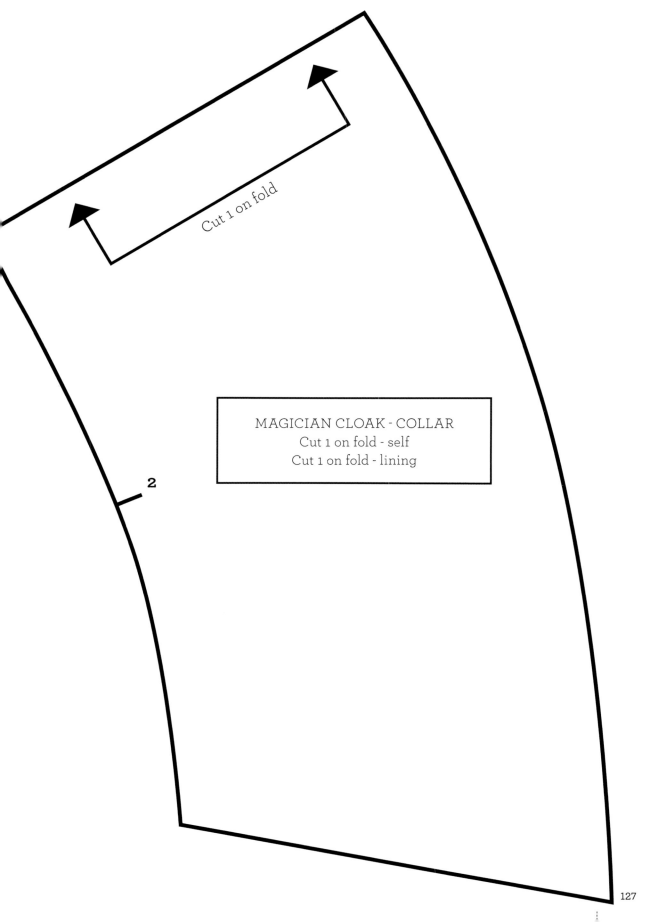

Cut 1 on fold

MAGICIAN CLOAK - COLLAR
Cut 1 on fold - self
Cut 1 on fold - lining

2

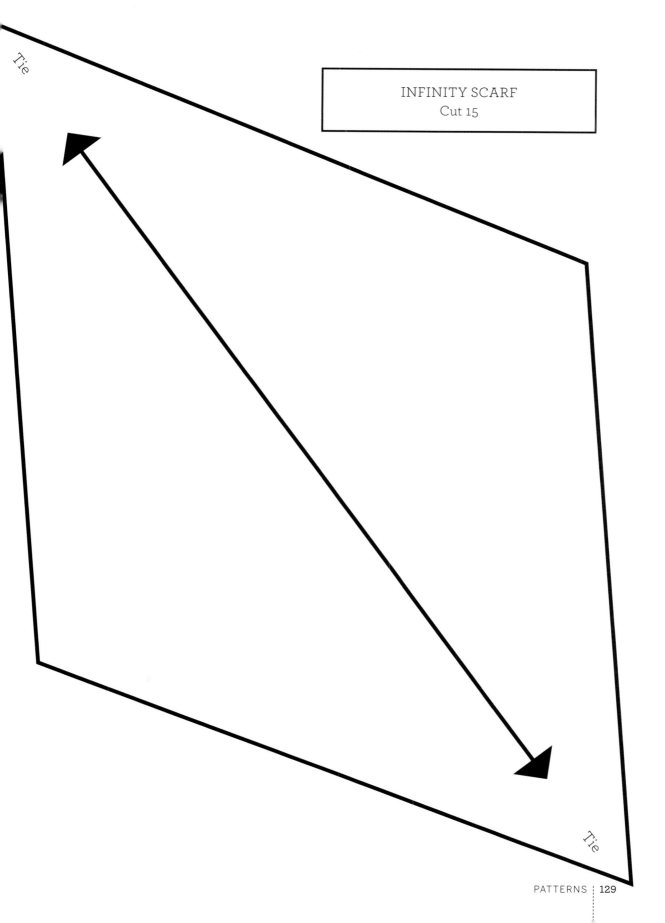

Tie

INFINITY SCARF
Cut 15

Tie

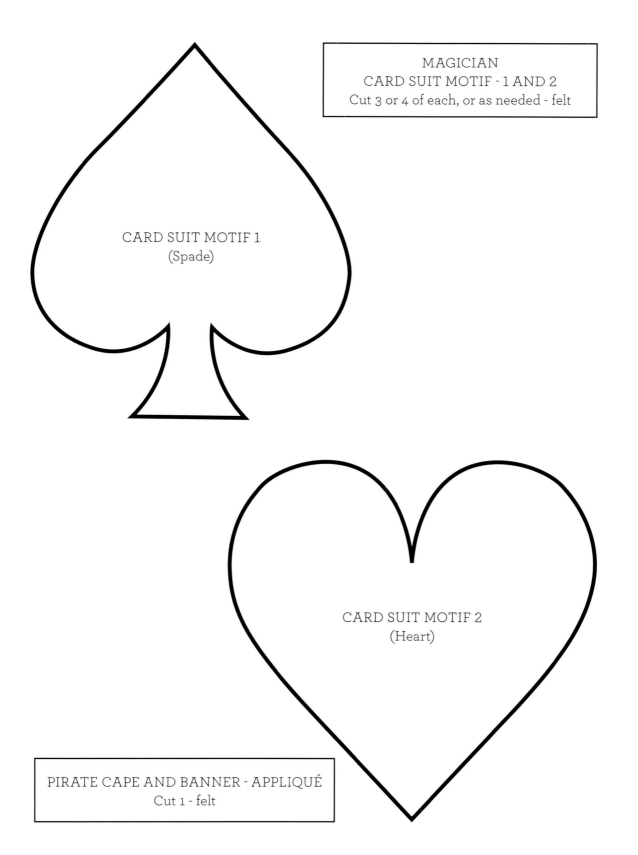

MAGICIAN
CARD SUIT MOTIF - 1 AND 2
Cut 3 or 4 of each, or as needed - felt

CARD SUIT MOTIF 1
(Spade)

CARD SUIT MOTIF 2
(Heart)

PIRATE CAPE AND BANNER - APPLIQUÉ
Cut 1 - felt

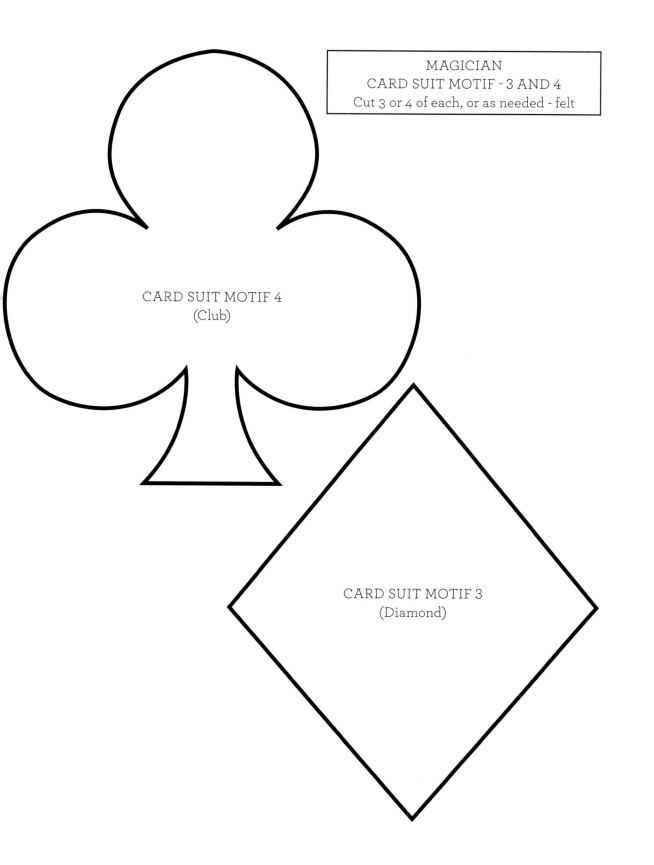

MAGICIAN
CARD SUIT MOTIF - 3 AND 4
Cut 3 or 4 of each, or as needed - felt

CARD SUIT MOTIF 4
(Club)

CARD SUIT MOTIF 3
(Diamond)

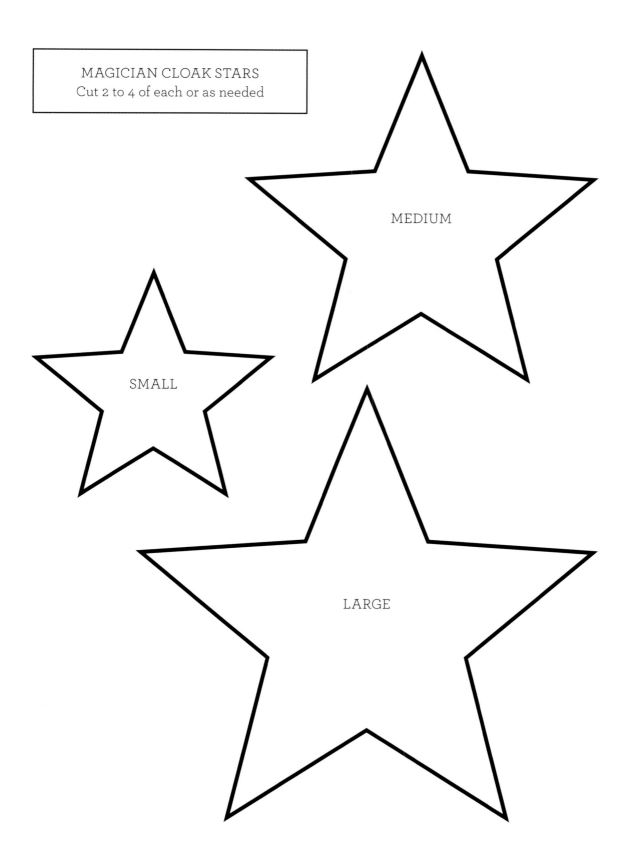

MAGICIAN CLOAK STARS
Cut 2 to 4 of each or as needed

MEDIUM

SMALL

LARGE

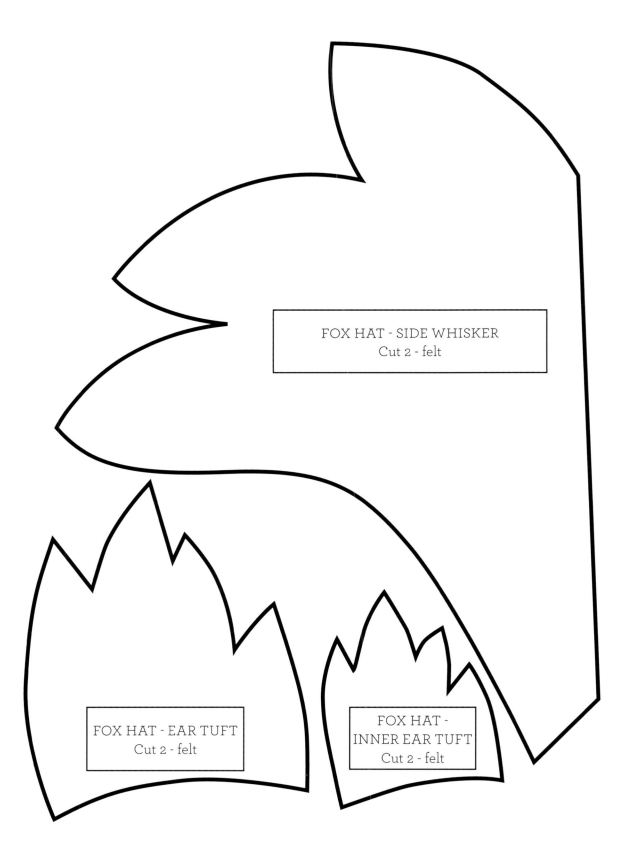

FOX HAT - SIDE WHISKER
Cut 2 - felt

FOX HAT - EAR TUFT
Cut 2 - felt

FOX HAT -
INNER EAR TUFT
Cut 2 - felt

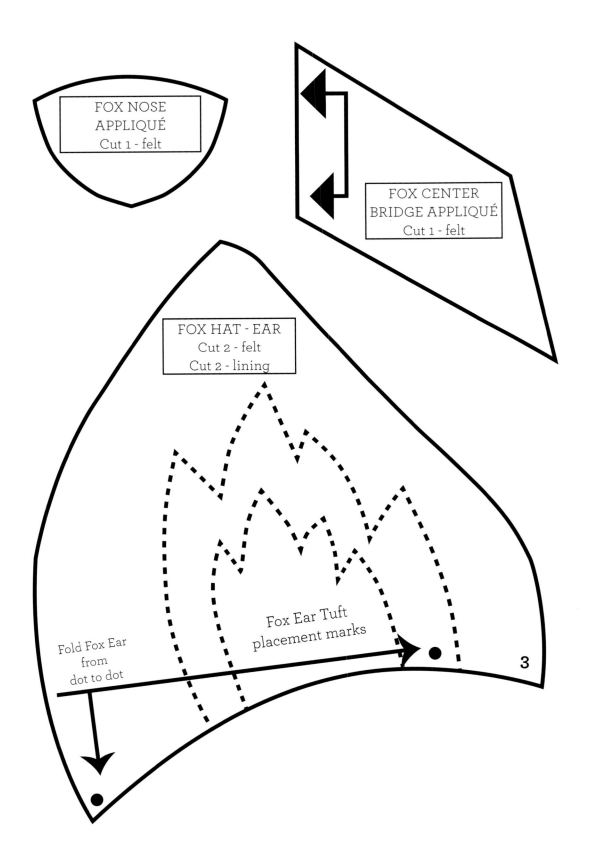

FOX NOSE
APPLIQUÉ
Cut 1 - felt

FOX CENTER
BRIDGE APPLIQUÉ
Cut 1 - felt

FOX HAT - EAR
Cut 2 - felt
Cut 2 - lining

Fox Ear Tuft
placement marks

Fold Fox Ear
from
dot to dot

3

resources

Recommended Supply Vendors

Etsy Studio. Etsy's craft supply market; look for the Etsy Studio
tag line (www.etsystudio.com)

Fabric.com. A great hub for all kinds of fabrics

Dritz. Notions of all kinds, ranging from pins to scissors to water soluble pens
(www.dritz.com)

Dick Blick. Tracing paper, pencils, pattern cardstock (www.dickblick.com)

Recommended Supplies

Coats and Clark. Thread, yarn, prints (available online through most major retailers)

Guttermans. Threads (available online through most major retailers)

HeatnBond Lite. (www.thermowebonline.com/c/our-brands_heatnbond)

Pellon. Quilt batting (www.pellonprojects.com)

Pacific Trimming. Velcro, Hook and Loop; many other decorative notions as well
(www.pacifictrimming.com)

Shop your local fabric stores and also check out thrift stores and rummage sales for truly
unique finished pieces.

Look in your own closet for well-loved pieces that have all those great memories: prints,
solids, canvas.

acknowledgments

Thank you to all of the little ones out there who love to dress up and dream big. Thank you to everyone who supports Lovelane Designs and handmade.

Many thanks to Joy Aquilino, Heather Godin, and Meredith Quinn at Creative Publishing international and Beth Baumgartel for your technical expertise. These ladies are the rock stars that made this book come to life.

High-fives and big gugs to the Lovelane team! Y'all are true MVPs. Paige, Jamie, Andrew, Tracy, Raquel, and the squish face brigade, Chugg, Pixie, and Lemmy: I love ya!

The kids are all right! Thank you to our awesome models and friends: Caroline, Cash, Chris, Emri, Henry, Liam, Sofia, and my darlin' Clementine. Additional wardrobe was provided by June and January (www.juneandjanuary.com). Miss Zoe Dog, Sophie, and Meredith: You belong in Hollywood.

A huge thank you to Lyn Bonham. Through your lens, this came together. It was a special treat to work on this project with you.

To my friends: thank you for being you. JLL, I always appreciate the last-minute homeruns.

Last, but definitely not least, a ginormous thank you to my family. Mom and Dad, your love and support have been unconditional from day one. Judy, you're the best MIL a gal could ask for! Patrick and Clementine, the two of you made this possible. I love you, times infinity.

about the author

Lane Huerta began dreaming and designing as an only child in rural North Carolina, where entertaining herself was the only option. Imagining adventures in the woods behind her house, she counts Pippi Longstocking and Punky Brewster as her earliest inspirations. In her teenage years, Lane attended the dynamic cloister of Boston's Walnut Hill School for the Arts, studying foundations and meeting creative kids from all over the world. After attending University of North Carolina School for the Arts, Lane landed in the cultural mecca of San Francisco. She refined the art and craft of graphic design with renowned rock poster designer Frank Kozik, along the way picking up the skill of screen-printing and a penchant for a bright, blocky aesthetic. A self-taught seamstress, Lane added textiles to her toolbox while working for international purse designer Mary Frances, who served as a creative business mentor and friend. A hankering for adventure led Lane to Savannah, Georgia, in 2006, where she set up shop as Lovelane Designs in the city's Landmark Historic District. She began designing and screen-printing tea towels, pillows, and other home décor, but it's been her imaginative children's designs that have captured the world's attention. Etsy featured Lovelane's children's wear on its home page, and Lane and her work have been featured on a variety of media outlets. Lane continues to work, live, and play in Savannah with her husband, Patrick, and her daughter, Clementine. Together, they imagine the most amazing adventures!

about the photographer

Lyn Bonham is a commercial and fine art photographer known for capturing the psychological moment that reveals the truth of relationships and the essence of an individual. She received her Master of Fine Arts degree in photography from the Savannah College of Art and Design. Her images are held in private collections, exhibited nationally, and published internationally. To view additional work, visit www.lynbonhamphotography.com.index

index